VIETNAM, CAMBODIA, LAOS & NORTHERN THAILAND TRAVEL GUIDE 2024-2025

A Trip to Hanoi, Ha long Bay, Ho Chi Minh City, Hoi An, Hue, Phnom Penh, Siem Reap, Sihanoukville, Vientiane, Luan Prabang, Bangkok, Chiang Mai, Chiang Rai, Sukhothai & Golden Triangle

By

JUDE K. BREMNER

WELCOME TO VIETNAM, CAMBODIA, LAOS & NORTHERN THAILAND

(Outer Map of the regions)

COPYRIGHT

DISCLAIMER

The information provided in this eBook, **"VIETNAM, CAMBODIA, LAOS & NORTHERN THAILAND TRAVEL GUIDE 2024-2025,"** authored by **Jude K. Bremner**, is intended for general informational purposes only. Readers are advised to use the content as a guide.

Legal Compliance

The author and publisher have made efforts to comply with copyright and intellectual property laws. If any inadvertent infringement is identified, it is unintentional, and the author encourages notification for prompt correction.

Conclusion:

"VIETNAM, CAMBODIA, LAOS & NORTHERN THAILAND TRAVEL GUIDE 2024-2025," is a tool for inspiration and planning, but it does not substitute personalized travel advice or professional consultation. Readers should exercise prudence and diligence in their travel endeavors.

By using this guide, readers acknowledge and accept the terms of this disclaimer. The author and publisher disclaim any liability for outcomes resulting from the use or interpretation of the information provided herein. **Travel safely and enjoy the wonders of Vietnam, Cambodia, Laos & Northern Thailand with an informed and discerning mindset.**

About The Author

Jude K. Bremner is the person who authored "VIETNAM, CAMBODIA, LAOS & NORTHERN TRAVEL GUIDE 2024-2025." **Jude** loves exploring different cultures and places, and he wants to share his excitement and knowledge with you through this guide.

A Passionate Traveler:

Jude started traveling to understand the unique stories of each place. He's been to bustling cities and Nations, remote landscapes, and hidden spots, all to discover what makes each destination special.

His Love for Vietnam, Cambodia, Laos & Northern Thailand:

Jude's love for **Vietnam, Cambodia, Laos & Northern Thailand** runs deep. Through multiple visits, he has immersed himself in the region's vibrant neighborhoods and pedaled along its scenic canals. **His encounters shape the authentic insights that make this guide an indispensable companion.**

Master of Insider Tips:

Jude is good at finding hidden gems and authentic experiences. **He wants to share these with you so you can have a memorable trip beyond the usual tourist spots.**

Author's Vision:

Jude's vision with this guide is to help you explore Vietnam, Cambodia, Laos & Northern Thailand like a pro. Exploring **Vietnam, Cambodia, Laos & Northern Thailand** like a pro means to dive into **its culture, history, and vibrant atmosphere,**

even without experiencing confusion in the long run or being worried about anything.

Let **Jude** be your reliable companion, unveiling the mysteries of **Vietnam, Cambodia, Laos & Northern Thailand** and ensuring your journey transcends mere travel, transforming into **a truly enriching experience.**

Table of Contents

- Ha Long Bay: Scenic cruises through limestone islands, kayaking, and cave visits
- Ho Chi Minh City (Saigon): War Remnants Museum, Notre-Dame Cathedral, and vibrant street life
- Hoi An: Lantern-lit streets, traditional crafts, and beaches
- Hue: The Imperial Citadel, ancient pagodas, and royal tombs
- Insider travel tips for Vietnam: transportation, cuisine, and local experiences

CHAPTER THREE: Cambodia

- Phnom Penh: Royal Palace, Silver Pagoda, Killing Fields, and Tuol Sleng Genocide Museum
- Siem Reap: Angkor Wat temple complex and sunrise views
- Sihanoukville: Beach escapes, nearby islands, and coastal relaxation
- Battambang: French colonial heritage, bamboo train, and countryside tours
- Insider travel tips for Cambodia: customs, language, and dining experiences

CHAPTER FOUR: Laos
- Luang Prabang: UNESCO-listed town, Mekong River, Kuang Si Falls, and traditional temples
- Vientiane: Patuxai Victory Monument, Pha That Luang, and Buddha Park
- Vang Vieng: Tubing, kayaking, limestone karsts, and cave explorations
- Si Phan Don (4,000 Islands): Mekong River islands, dolphins, and laid-back charm
- Insider travel tips for Laos: cultural etiquette, must-try dishes, and transportation

CHAPTER FIVE: Northern Thailand
- Chiang Mai: Temples, night markets, and hill tribe villages
- Chiang Rai: The White Temple, Blue Temple, and Golden Triangle exploration
- Sukhothai: Ancient capital
- Mae Hong Son: Mountain landscapes, Pai Canyon, and cultural experiences
- Insider travel tips for Northern Thailand: local traditions, best hiking spots, and cuisine

CHAPTER SIX: 7-Day Itinerary
- Day 1: Hanoi, Vietnam
- Day 2: Ha Long Bay, Vietnam
- Day 3: Phnom Penh, Cambodia
- Day 4: Siem Reap, Cambodia
- Day 5: Luang Prabang, Laos
- Day 6: Chiang Mai, Thailand
- Day 7: Chiang Rai & Golden Triangle, Thailand

CHAPTER SEVEN: Practical Information & Resources for Travelers
- Recommended accommodations
- Local transportation options
- Key phrases in Vietnamese, Khmer, Lao, and Thai
- Packing guide for Southeast Asia
- Health tips
- Additional resources

OTHER BOOKS RECOMMENDATION
A KIND GESTURE.

Chapter One:

Introduction to Vietnam, Cambodia, Laos & Northern Thailand

Overview of Southeast Asia's charm and cultural diversity

Southeast Asia is a part of the world that attracts many travelers because of its rich history, stunning natural landscapes, and warm, friendly people. This region is made up of many countries, but four of the most popular destinations for visitors are Vietnam, Cambodia, Laos, and Northern Thailand.

Each of these places has its own unique culture and traditions, but they also share similarities, making them an exciting group of countries to visit in one trip.

• The Blend of Old and New

One of the most remarkable things about Southeast Asia is the way old traditions and modern life blend together. In cities like Hanoi (Vietnam) and Phnom Penh (Cambodia), you can see bustling streets with motorbikes zooming by tall buildings, while right around the corner, you might find ancient temples or quiet markets where time seems to stand still.

In Northern Thailand, for example, the city of Chiang Mai is known for its temples and religious festivals, but it's also a modern city where you can find restaurants serving international food, coffee shops, and even night markets selling trendy clothes and gadgets. The same goes for Luang Prabang in Laos, where beautiful old temples sit alongside French colonial buildings, showing how history and present-day life coexist.

• **Natural Beauty**

The natural beauty of Southeast Asia is another big reason people come to visit. From the breathtaking limestone cliffs in Ha Long Bay, Vietnam, to the peaceful rivers and mountains in Laos, there is always something amazing to see.

Sihanoukville in Cambodia offers sandy beaches and clear blue waters, perfect for anyone who loves the ocean. Meanwhile, the Mekong River, which flows through several countries, is a source of life and culture for many people in the region.

In Northern Thailand, you can experience the mountains and lush green forests, which are home to many types of plants and animals. Travelers who like adventure often visit Chiang Rai or trek through the Golden

Triangle, where Thailand meets Laos and Myanmar, to explore the countryside.

• **A Rich Cultural History**

Southeast Asia has a deep cultural history that is reflected in its temples, ancient ruins, and festivals. One of the most famous examples is Angkor Wat in Cambodia, an ancient temple complex that is one of the largest religious monuments in the world. It was built over 900 years ago and still stands today as a symbol of the Khmer Empire.

In Vietnam, you can visit places like the Imperial City of Hue, which was once the capital of the country. This city is filled with old palaces, tombs, and temples, all of which tell the story of Vietnam's past. Laos also has its own unique history, with Luang Prabang being a UNESCO World Heritage site. This town is famous for its well-preserved architecture and the many monks who live there.

Northern Thailand has a strong cultural identity, too. Cities like Sukhothai have ancient ruins that show what life was like in the past, while festivals like Yi Peng (the lantern festival) in Chiang Mai allow visitors to see traditional customs in action.

• **Welcoming People and Delicious Food**

One of the best things about traveling in Southeast Asia is the friendliness of the people. Whether you're in the busy streets of Ho Chi Minh City or in a small village in Laos, you will often be greeted with a smile. The people of this region are known for being kind and welcoming to travelers, and many will go out of their way to make sure you have a good experience.

Another highlight of visiting Southeast Asia is the food. Each country has its own special dishes that reflect the flavors and ingredients of the area. In Vietnam, you can enjoy pho, a noodle soup that's both light and flavorful, or banh mi, a delicious sandwich with French and Vietnamese influences. In Thailand, famous dishes like pad thai and green curry are a must-try, while Cambodia offers tasty meals like amok, a traditional fish dish cooked in banana leaves. Laos is known for laap, a minced meat salad often served with sticky rice.

• **Spirituality and Traditions**

Many people in Southeast Asia follow Buddhism, and this religion plays a big role in the daily lives of the people.

You will see temples everywhere, where monks live and practice their faith. Visitors are often welcomed to visit these temples, where they can learn about Buddhism and even join in meditation sessions.

In countries like Laos and Northern Thailand, the sight of monks walking down the street early in the morning, collecting offerings from the local people, is a common one.

This tradition, called alms giving, is a way for people to earn good merit and show respect to the monks.

• **Vibrant Festivals**

Southeast Asia is also known for its vibrant festivals that happen throughout the year. In Cambodia, the Water Festival is one of the biggest events, where people celebrate with boat races and fireworks to mark the end of the rainy season.

Thailand is famous for its Songkran Festival, which is the Thai New Year and is celebrated with water fights across the country. In Laos, the Boun Pi Mai (New Year) festival is similar, with water blessings and traditional dances.

These festivals are a great way for travelers to experience the local culture and join in the fun.

• **A Place for Every Traveler**

Whether you're an adventurer looking to trek through jungles and mountains, a history lover eager to explore ancient temples and ruins, or someone who just wants to relax on a beach, Southeast Asia offers something for everyone. The combination of natural beauty, cultural richness, delicious food, and kind-hearted people makes this part of the world a truly special place to visit.

Brief history and cultural background of the region

Vietnam, Cambodia, Laos, and Northern Thailand are countries that has been shaped by ancient kingdoms, colonial rule, wars, and cultural exchanges with other parts of the world. Today, they each have unique cultures, but they also share many similarities that link them together. Let's explore the history and culture of this fascinating region.

• **Early Civilizations and Kingdoms**

Thousands of years ago, powerful kingdoms and empires ruled this region. Vietnam has a history that dates back over 4,000 years, starting with the ancient kingdom of Van Lang, which is considered the first Vietnamese state. Over time, Vietnam was influenced by China, which ruled parts of the country for nearly 1,000 years. This led to the adoption of Chinese writing, religion (like Buddhism and Confucianism), and government systems.

Cambodia was once home to one of the greatest empires in Southeast Asia, the Khmer Empire. This empire ruled from the 9th to the 15th centuries and built the famous Angkor Wat, the largest religious monument in the world. The Khmer Empire was known for its advanced engineering, especially in building complex irrigation systems and massive stone temples. The people of Cambodia followed Hinduism before eventually adopting Buddhism, which remains the main religion today.

Laos was once part of the Lan Xang Kingdom, which means "Land of a Million Elephants." This kingdom was founded in the 14th century and was a powerful force in the region for several hundred years. Buddhism became the dominant religion in Laos during this time, and it influenced the building of many temples and religious practices that are still seen today.

Northern Thailand, home to cities like Chiang Mai and Chiang Rai, was historically part of the Lanna Kingdom. The Lanna Kingdom flourished from the 13th to the 18th centuries, and its influence can still be seen today in the architecture and traditions of Northern Thailand. Like Laos and Cambodia, Buddhism played a significant role in shaping the culture of this region.

• **Colonial Rule and Independence**

In the 19th century, European powers began to take control of much of Southeast Asia. Vietnam, Cambodia, and Laos became part of French Indochina in the late 1800s. The French ruled over these countries, influencing their architecture, education systems, and economies. While the French introduced new ways of life, the people of these countries still kept many of their traditional customs and beliefs.

During this time, Northern Thailand remained independent, though the entire country of Thailand (then known as Siam) faced pressure from both the British and

French. Unlike its neighbors, Thailand managed to avoid being colonized by signing treaties with European countries, allowing it to stay free while making compromises to avoid conflict.

In the 20th century, Vietnam, Cambodia, and Laos fought for their independence from the French. Vietnam was the first to gain independence, but this led to the Vietnam War, a conflict between the communist North Vietnam and the non-communist South Vietnam, which was supported by the United States. After years of fighting, the war ended in 1975 with North Vietnam taking control of the whole country, forming the Socialist Republic of Vietnam.

Cambodia also gained its independence in 1953, but the country soon faced internal conflict. In the 1970s, a group called the Khmer Rouge, led by Pol Pot, took control of Cambodia and caused a tragic period known as the Cambodian Genocide. During this time, millions of people were killed or died from starvation and disease. The country eventually recovered, but the effects of this dark time are still felt today.

Laos also became independent in 1953 but experienced a civil war that ended with the rise of a communist government in 1975. Like Vietnam, Laos is now a socialist state, though it has slowly opened up to the world in recent decades.

• Cultural Influence of Religion

Religion plays a very important role in the cultural identity of Vietnam, Cambodia, Laos, and Northern Thailand. Buddhism is the most common religion across all these countries, but each nation has its own style and practices.

In Vietnam, Buddhism is mixed with Taoism and Confucianism, creating a unique blend of beliefs known as the Three Teachings. Many Vietnamese people visit pagodas and temples to pray for good fortune, health, and happiness, and you'll see festivals and rituals that honor both Buddhist and traditional gods and ancestors.

In Cambodia, Buddhism became the state religion after the fall of the Khmer Empire. Almost every village in Cambodia has a pagoda, where monks live and practice. The Cambodian people often visit these pagodas to make offerings and pray for blessings.

Laos is known for its quiet and peaceful way of life, and Buddhism is central to this. Monks in orange robes can be seen collecting alms (food offerings) in the early mornings, and temples in cities like Luang Prabang are important centers for both religion and community life.

In Northern Thailand, Buddhism also plays a key role. Chiang Mai, known as the cultural capital of Northern Thailand, is home to hundreds of temples, each with its own history. Festivals like Loy Krathong and Yi Peng, where people float lanterns and make offerings to the water spirits, show how deeply connected religion is to daily life in Thailand.

• Language and Art

The languages spoken in these countries reflect their history and culture. Vietnamese has many words borrowed from Chinese due to centuries of Chinese rule, while also being influenced by French during colonial times. In Cambodia, the Khmer language is widely spoken, and its script is unique to the region, with roots in ancient Sanskrit. Lao, spoken in Laos, shares similarities with Thai, as the two languages come from the same linguistic family.

Art and music in these countries are also influenced by their religious beliefs and historical experiences. In Vietnam, traditional water puppetry tells stories of everyday life and folklore, while Cambodian Apsara dance, a form of classical dance, reflects the grandeur of the ancient Khmer Empire. Laos is known for its bamboo weaving and intricate textiles, often made with natural dyes and traditional patterns. In Northern Thailand, Lanna-style temples and handmade crafts are reminders of the region's rich artistic heritage.

• **Festivals and Traditions**

Festivals are an important part of life in Southeast Asia, and each country has its own special celebrations that reflect its history and culture. In Vietnam, Tet (the Lunar New Year) is the biggest festival of the year, marking the arrival of spring and the start of a new year. People visit their families, clean their houses, and offer prayers for a prosperous year.

In Cambodia, the Water Festival marks the end of the rainy season and is celebrated with boat races and fireworks. Laos celebrates the Lao New Year with water blessings, parades, and traditional music. In Northern Thailand, the Songkran Festival (Thai New Year) is famous for its water fights, where people throw water on each other to wash away the past year's bad luck.

These festivals are not just fun; they are also deeply rooted in the countries' religious and cultural traditions, making them a meaningful way for people to connect with their heritage.

Travel trends and why visit in 2024-2025

Let's take a look at the travel trends for 2024-2025 and why visiting these countries during this period will be a rewarding experience.

• Sustainable Travel and Ecotourism

In recent years, more and more travelers are becoming concerned about the impact of tourism on the environment. As a result, sustainable travel and ecotourism have grown in popularity. This means travelers are looking for ways to enjoy nature without causing harm to the environment.

Vietnam, Cambodia, Laos, and Northern Thailand are ideal places for this type of travel because they offer many natural attractions that can be explored in eco-friendly ways. For example, travelers can take boat tours through the Mekong River in a sustainable way, stay in eco-lodges in the mountains of Northern Thailand, or visit wildlife sanctuaries in Laos where animals are protected. In Vietnam, national parks like Phong Nha-Ke Bang offer guided tours that educate visitors about nature conservation.

In 2024-2025, more eco-friendly accommodations, like hotels using solar power and farms practicing sustainable agriculture, will open up in these countries. Travelers can enjoy beautiful natural sites while knowing they are supporting businesses that care for the planet.

- **Remote Work and Digital Nomads**

During the COVID-19 pandemic, the way in which people across many Nations work changed entirely. More people are now able to work from anywhere, which has led to the rise of digital nomads—people who travel while working remotely. Southeast Asia, especially places like Northern Thailand, has become a popular choice for these remote workers due to its affordable living costs, fast internet, and welcoming communities.

Chiang Mai in Northern Thailand, in particular, has become a hotspot for digital nomads. The city has modern coworking spaces, great street food, and lots of activities to enjoy in your free time. In 2024-2025, the trend of remote work is expected to continue, and more cities in the region, like Hanoi in Vietnam and Vientiane in Laos, may also see an increase in digital nomads. The relaxed lifestyle, beautiful surroundings, and lower cost of living make these countries an attractive option for those looking to combine work and travel.

• Authentic Cultural Experiences

Travelers today are looking for more authentic experiences when they visit a new place. They don't just want to see the famous sights; they also want to learn about local traditions, meet local people, and understand how they live. In 2024-2025, this trend will continue to grow, and Vietnam, Cambodia, Laos, and Northern Thailand are great places to experience local culture in a meaningful way.

For example, in Hoi An (Vietnam), visitors can participate in traditional lantern-making workshops and take a cooking class to learn how to make local dishes like pho and banh mi. In Luang Prabang (Laos), tourists can give alms to the monks early in the morning, which is a long-standing tradition in the country. Similarly, in Cambodia, visitors can experience the life of a farmer by visiting local rice farms or spend time learning about traditional crafts like silk weaving.

These countries are also home to many festivals where visitors can join in the celebrations. The Water Festival in Cambodia and Songkran (Thai New Year) in Thailand are examples of cultural events that welcome travelers to participate in local customs. Visiting during these times will allow tourists to connect with local people and better understand their culture.

• **Adventure Travel**

For those who love outdoor activities and adventure, Vietnam, Cambodia, Laos, and Northern Thailand offer plenty of opportunities. Adventure travel is another growing trend, and it's expected to continue gaining popularity in 2024-2025. Many travelers are looking for exciting activities like hiking, cycling, kayaking, and even caving.

In Vietnam, Ha Long Bay is a top destination for kayaking, while the northern mountains, like those around Sapa, are perfect for trekking through rice terraces and visiting ethnic villages. In Laos, the Nam Song River offers opportunities for tubing, and there are plenty of mountain biking trails around Vang Vieng. Cambodia's Cardamom Mountains provide a great location for jungle treks, and in Northern Thailand, travelers can trek through national parks like Doi Inthanon, which is home to the highest mountain in Thailand.

These adventure activities allow travelers to see the natural beauty of the region while staying active and experiencing thrilling challenges.

• **Culinary Travel**

One of the biggest reasons to visit Southeast Asia is for its food. Culinary travel, or traveling to experience the local food and drink, is a trend that is growing quickly. In 2024-2025, more travelers will be seeking out local food markets, street food stalls, and cooking classes as part of their trip.

Vietnam is known for its flavorful dishes like pho (noodle soup) and spring rolls, and many visitors love trying the street food in cities like Ho Chi Minh City and Hanoi. Cambodia has its own special dishes, such as amok, a coconut milk-based curry, and nom banh chok, a traditional rice noodle dish. Laos is famous for larb, a spicy minced meat salad, and sticky rice, while Northern Thailand offers dishes like khao soi, a coconut curry noodle soup, and spicy som tam (papaya salad).

In addition to eating at restaurants and food stalls, more travelers are signing up for food tours or cooking classes to learn how to make these traditional dishes themselves. This hands-on experience gives visitors a deeper connection to the local culture and makes their trip even more memorable.

• **Wellness and Spiritual Travel**

Wellness tourism is another trend that has been growing steadily and is expected to continue rising in 2024-2025. Many people are looking for ways to improve their health and well-being while traveling. The region's connection to Buddhism and its peaceful landscapes make it a perfect destination for travelers seeking inner peace and relaxation.

In Northern Thailand, there are many meditation retreats and yoga centers where visitors can spend a few days or even weeks focusing on their mental and physical health. Laos and Cambodia also have wellness resorts offering everything from traditional herbal treatments to spa therapies. Vietnam,

47

especially in places like Hoi An, is seeing a rise in wellness tourism with yoga classes, meditation retreats, and spa resorts.

These wellness experiences allow travelers to slow down, connect with nature, and rejuvenate during their trip.

• Improved Accessibility and Infrastructure

One of the reasons Southeast Asia is expected to see more tourists in 2024-2025 is the improvement in travel infrastructure. Over the past few years, airports, roads, and train services have been upgraded, making it easier to travel between cities and countries in the region. New flight routes have been added between Vietnam, Cambodia, Laos, and Thailand, reducing travel time and costs.

For example, the new high-speed train from Bangkok to Chiang Mai allows visitors to travel faster between these two major cities.

Vietnam has also been improving its railways, and Cambodia is working on upgrading its roads to make travel more convenient for tourists.

These improvements make it easier for travelers to explore multiple countries during one trip, taking advantage of the cultural diversity and natural beauty that the region offers.

Practical travel tips

When planning a trip to Vietnam, Cambodia, Laos, and Northern Thailand, it's important to be prepared with practical travel tips. Knowing about visas, currency, transportation, and safety will help you have a smooth and enjoyable journey. Here are some important information to keep in mind as you travel:

• **Visas**

Each country has different visa rules, so it's important to check before you travel.

- Vietnam:

Most tourists need a visa to enter Vietnam. However, citizens from some countries (like the UK, Germany, France, and a few others) can visit visa-free for a short stay (usually 15 days or less). You can apply for a visa on arrival (VOA) online, but you must get an approval letter first. There is also an e-visa option available for people from certain countries, which allows you to stay for up to 30 days.

- Cambodia:

For Cambodia, a visa on arrival is available at airports and border crossings for most nationalities. You can also apply for an e-visa online. Both options typically allow a stay of up to 30 days.

- Laos:

Laos also offers a visa on arrival for most visitors, which is valid for 30 days. You can get it at the airport or land borders. There is also an e-visa option available, which can be applied for online before your trip.

- Thailand:

Visitors travelling to Thailand from many countries will have the opportunity to stay for up to 30 days without a visa. Yes! If you need to stay longer, you can apply for a visa on arrival or extend your stay at an immigration office.

Always check the latest requirements before traveling because visa rules can change. It's also important to have at least six months of validity on your passport.

• **Currency**

Each of the Countries uses a different currency for payment and transactions.

- Vietnam:

Vietnamese dong is the official currency people living in Vietnam do make use of. ATMs are widely available in major cities, and you can easily exchange money at banks or currency exchange counters. Credit cards are accepted in many hotels and restaurants, but cash is preferred in smaller shops and rural areas.

- Cambodia:

The Cambodian riel (KHR) is the official currency people living in Cambodia do make use of. Although, the US dollar is widely accepted and often used for larger purchases. In fact, many transactions in tourist areas are quoted in dollars. It's common to receive change in both riel and dollars.

- Laos:

The Lao kip (LAK) is the official currency for people living in Laos. You can exchange foreign currency at banks and exchange offices. ATMs are available in larger cities, but they can be less reliable in rural areas, so it's a good idea to carry some cash with you.

- Thailand:

In Thailand, Thai baht is a currency that is generally used there for any form of transaction or payment. ATMs are easy to find in most towns and cities, and credit cards are accepted in many hotels, restaurants, and stores. However, smaller shops and markets often prefer cash.

It's always a good idea to carry a mix of cash and cards, and to have some local currency on hand for small purchases or when visiting rural areas.

• Transportation

Getting around in Vietnam, Cambodia, Laos, and Northern Thailand can be done in various ways, depending on your preferences and budget.

- Flights:

Domestic flights are a good option if you're short on time. There are several low-cost airlines that operate in the region, making it easy to fly between major cities like Hanoi, Ho Chi Minh City, Phnom Penh, Vientiane, and Bangkok. You can also fly between countries, but keep in mind that some smaller airports may have fewer flight options.

- Buses:

Buses are the most common form of transport and are often the cheapest way to travel between cities and towns. Long-distance buses are available, but travel times can be long, especially in mountainous areas. In Vietnam and Thailand, there are sleeper buses for overnight journeys.

- Trains:

In Vietnam and Thailand, the train is a comfortable way to travel long distances. The Reunification Express in Vietnam runs between Hanoi and Ho Chi Minh City, offering different classes of service.

In Thailand, trains run from Bangkok to Northern Thailand, including Chiang Mai. Trains are slower than buses but can offer a more scenic and relaxed journey.

- Tuk-tuks and motorbikes:

In cities, tuk-tuks and motorbike taxis are popular forms of transport. You can also rent motorbikes in many areas, but make sure to wear a helmet and be aware of local driving conditions.

- Boats:

In places like Ha Long Bay (Vietnam) or the Mekong River (Cambodia/Laos), boat travel is a great way to see the countryside. There are also ferry services in Northern Thailand that cross the Mekong River to Laos.

• Safety

The region is generally safe for tourists, but it's always good to take some basic precautions:

- Petty theft:

Be aware of your belongings in crowded areas or when using public transportation.

Pickpocketing can happen in busy markets or tourist spots.

- Health:

The good thing here is this: it's advisable to have travel insurance that covers for health concerns. Ensure you stay cautious. Also try to avoid street food and drink only bottled water you're sure of.

Vaccinations for diseases like typhoid and hepatitis may be recommended before traveling.

- Traffic safety:

In some areas, traffic can be chaotic, especially in major cities like Hanoi and Phnom Penh.

Always be careful when crossing the street and consider using taxis or rideshare services if you're unsure about renting a motorbike.

- Cultural respect:

Be mindful of local customs. It's polite to greet people with a slight bow or a smile, as this is a common way of showing respect in the region.

Best times to visit

The best time to visit Vietnam, Cambodia, Laos, and Northern Thailand depends on what kind of weather you prefer and which activities you plan to do.

The region has a tropical climate, with wet and dry seasons that can vary from country to country.

Here's a guide to help you plan your trip based on the seasons.

• **Vietnam**

- The Northern region or division of Vietnam (e.g Sapa, Hanoi, Ha Long Bay):

The best time to visit is during the spring (March to April) and autumn (September to November). During these times, the weather is pleasant, with cooler temperatures and less rain. The summer months (June to August) can be very hot and rainy, while winter (December to February) can be chilly, especially in the mountains around Sapa.

- The Central region or division of Vietnam (e.g Da Nang, Hoi An, Hue):

The ideal time for any visitor visiting these locations is from February to May. During this period, the weather is warm and dry as well. Avoid the rainy season (September to November), when there is a higher risk of typhoons and heavy rainfall.

- The Southern region or division of Vietnam (e.g Mekong Delta, Ho Chi Minh City):

The best time to visit is during the dry season (December to April), when temperatures are warm but not too humid. The rainy season (May to November) brings frequent downpours, but they are often short and happen in the afternoon.

• **Cambodia**

Cambodia experiences a similar climate to Southern Vietnam. The best time to visit is during the cool and dry season from November to February, when the temperatures are more comfortable, and the humidity is lower. This is a great time to visit Angkor Wat and explore the temples without the intense heat.

The wet season (June to October) brings heavy rainfall, but the countryside becomes lush and green. It's also a less crowded time to visit, and the rain showers are usually short.

• Laos

The best time to visit Laos is from November to February when the weather is cooler and dry. This is the peak tourist season, especially in places like Luang Prabang and the Plain of Jars.

The wet season (May to October) brings high humidity and regular rain, but it also makes the rivers full and waterfalls more impressive.

If you don't mind a bit of rain, visiting during this time can be rewarding.

• **Northern Thailand**

Northern Thailand has three main seasons:

- Cool season (November to February):

This is the best time to visit, with cool mornings and evenings, making it perfect for trekking and exploring cities like Chiang Mai and Chiang Rai.

This is also the time of major festivals like Loi Krathong.

- Hot season (March to May):

Temperatures can rise significantly, especially in April, making outdoor activities more challenging.

- Rainy season (June to October):

Expect frequent showers, but the countryside turns green, and there are fewer tourists. The rain usually comes in short bursts, so it's still possible to enjoy sightseeing.

Chapter Two: Vietnam

Hanoi

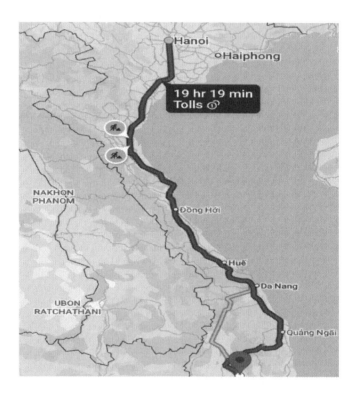

• The map above shows distance (with time covered) from Vietnam central area to Hanoi

Hanoi, the capital of Vietnam, is a city that perfectly blends history with modern life. As the political center of the country, it is where important decisions are made, and it is home to government offices and the residence of the president. But beyond its political importance, Hanoi is also rich in culture, filled with traditional markets, ancient temples, and French colonial buildings that tell stories of the city's past.

• Cultural and Political Capital

Hanoi has been the heart of Vietnam for over a thousand years. The city's history dates back to 1010, when it was first chosen as the capital of ancient Vietnam. Through the years, it has seen many changes, from being ruled by emperors to being colonized by the French. Today, it stands as a symbol of Vietnam's strength and independence. It's where you'll find key political sites, such as the Ho Chi Minh Mausoleum, where the country's most famous leader, Ho Chi Minh, is honored. His impact on Vietnam's fight for independence can be felt throughout the city, and his resting place is a major landmark visited by locals and tourists alike.

As a cultural capital, Hanoi is also the center of Vietnamese traditions, art, and cuisine. From ancient festivals to modern art galleries, the city reflects the diversity and creativity of the Vietnamese people. Whether it's the traditional music performances, water puppetry shows, or street food markets, there is always something happening that gives you a taste of local life.

• Old Quarter

One of the most exciting areas of Hanoi is the Old Quarter. It is the oldest part of the city, and it's known for its narrow streets filled with shops, markets, and houses that have been there for hundreds of years. Walking through the Old Quarter feels like stepping back in time, as the streets are named after the goods that were once sold there. For example, Hang Gai Street is known for selling silk, while Hang Bac Street is famous for its silver jewelry.

The Old Quarter is a maze of small streets and alleyways, where you can discover traditional craft shops, street food vendors, and historical sites like ancient temples and pagodas. One of the highlights of the Old Quarter is the Dong Xuan Market, a large indoor market where you can find everything from fresh produce to souvenirs. It's a busy, noisy place where locals haggle over prices and tourists can shop for unique items to take home.

Despite the hustle and bustle, the Old Quarter also has a peaceful side, especially in the early mornings when local residents practice tai chi or go for quiet walks. The area is known for its sense of community, and many families have lived there for generations, passing down their homes and businesses from one family member to the next.

• Hoan Kiem Lake

Right next to the Old Quarter is Hoan Kiem Lake, one of the most beautiful and peaceful spots in Hanoi. The lake is surrounded by trees, walking paths, and benches, making it a popular place for both locals and tourists to relax. The name Hoan Kiem means "Lake of the Returned Sword," and there is a famous legend that goes along with it. According to the story, a great Vietnamese king received a magical sword from a giant turtle in the lake, which he used to fight off foreign invaders. After the battle was won, the turtle took the sword back into the lake, and it has been a symbol of Vietnamese strength and unity ever since.

In the middle of Hoan Kiem Lake is Turtle Tower, a small structure that stands on an island. While it's not open to visitors, the tower adds to the charm of the lake, and many people come to take pictures of it. Another famous landmark near the lake is the Ngoc Son Temple, which sits on a different island and can be reached by crossing the Red Bridge. The temple is dedicated to General Tran Hung Dao, who helped defend Vietnam from the Mongols in the 13th century. It's a peaceful place where visitors can learn more about the country's history while enjoying the view of the lake.

Hoan Kiem Lake is more than just a tourist spot—it's a part of daily life in Hanoi. In the mornings, you'll see people exercising, jogging, and practicing traditional martial arts around the lake. In the evenings, families gather to stroll and enjoy the cool breeze. On weekends, the streets around the lake are closed to traffic, and it becomes a lively pedestrian zone with music, street performances, and food stalls.

• French Colonial Architecture

One of the unique aspects of Hanoi is its mix of architectural styles, which reflect its rich history. During the time when Vietnam was colonized by the French, many buildings were constructed in the French colonial style. Today, these buildings add a European touch to the city, with their grand facades, large windows, and elegant details. Walking through Hanoi, you'll see many examples of French colonial architecture, especially in the French Quarter, which is located near Hoan Kiem Lake.

Some of the most iconic buildings in the city include the Hanoi Opera House, which looks similar to the Opera House in Paris. The building was completed in 1911, and it remains one of the most important cultural venues in the city. Today, it hosts concerts, ballets, and other performances, allowing visitors to experience both Vietnamese and international art.

Another famous example of French colonial architecture is St. Joseph's Cathedral, which was built in 1886. The cathedral's design is inspired by Notre-Dame Cathedral in Paris, with its tall spires and Gothic style. St. Joseph's Cathedral is still an active church, and visitors can attend services or simply admire its beauty from the outside.

The French colonial influence is also seen in Hanoi's government buildings, hotels, and villas, many of which have been preserved and are still in use today. The mix of traditional Vietnamese and French architecture gives the city a unique charm that sets it apart from other capitals in Southeast Asia.

Ha Long Bay

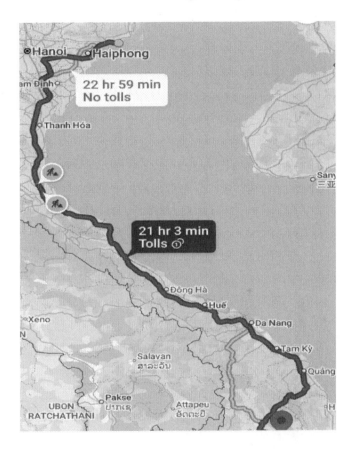

- The map above shows distance (with time covered) from Vietnam central area to Ha long Bay

Ha Long Bay, located in northern Vietnam, is one of the country's most beautiful natural wonders. Known for its towering limestone islands and emerald-green waters, it's a place where visitors can relax and enjoy the stunning scenery while taking part in a variety of fun activities. From cruising through the bay to kayaking and exploring hidden caves, Ha Long Bay offers something for everyone, whether you're seeking adventure or just looking for a peaceful retreat.

• **Scenic Cruises Through Limestone Islands**

One of the best ways to experience Ha Long Bay is by taking a scenic cruise. As the boat glides through the calm waters, you'll be surrounded by nearly 2,000 limestone islands and islets. These islands, which rise dramatically from the sea, have been shaped by millions of years of wind and water erosion, giving them unique shapes and making them a breathtaking sight.

Cruises in Ha Long Bay range from short day trips to overnight stays, allowing visitors to fully appreciate the beauty of the area. Some of the islands are covered in lush green forests, while others are bare rock formations. The boats slowly weave between the islands, giving passengers plenty of time to take photos, admire the scenery, and enjoy the tranquility of the bay.

Many of the cruises include stops at some of the larger islands, where visitors can get off the boat and explore.

Some cruises even offer the chance to visit floating fishing villages, where people live on the water and make their living by fishing. It's a fascinating glimpse into a way of life that has been part of Ha Long Bay for generations.

• Kayaking in Ha Long Bay

For those looking to get a bit closer to the water, kayaking is a popular activity in Ha Long Bay. While cruising allows you to see the islands from a distance, kayaking lets you explore the bay at your own pace. You can paddle around the base of towering limestone cliffs, glide through quiet lagoons, and even venture into hidden caves that are too small for larger boats to enter.

Kayaking is an adventure that offers a new perspective of Ha Long Bay. As you paddle through the water, you'll feel the peace and quiet of the bay. Many kayakers are able to get closer to the wildlife that lives in the area, such as birds that nest on the rocky cliffs or fish swimming in the clear waters below.

Some parts of Ha Long Bay are only accessible by kayak, making it a special way to explore. For example, there are small caves and hidden lagoons that open up into secret beaches or peaceful pools of water, surrounded by cliffs. These spots are not always easy to find, but with a kayak, you can reach them and enjoy the untouched beauty of the bay.

• **Cave Visits**

Another highlight of Ha Long Bay is the chance to explore its many caves. These caves, formed over millions of years, are hidden within the limestone islands and offer visitors the opportunity to go underground and see the impressive rock formations inside.

One of the most famous caves in Ha Long Bay is the Sung Sot Cave, also known as the Surprise Cave. As the name suggests, visitors are often surprised by the size of the cave and the beauty of its interior. The cave is made up of two large chambers, with the first chamber resembling a giant auditorium and the second chamber filled with stunning stalactites and stalagmites. Visitors can walk through the cave on a designated path, which is well-lit to showcase the natural formations.

Another popular cave is the Thien Cung Cave, also known as the Heavenly Palace Cave. This cave is famous for its intricate rock formations, which seem to resemble scenes from an ancient legend. The walls of the cave are decorated with delicate stalactites that hang from the ceiling, while the floor is dotted with stalagmites. Some formations are said to look like dragons, phoenixes, and other mythical creatures, adding to the magical atmosphere of the cave.

Cave visits are typically included as part of a cruise or day trip, and they offer a fascinating look at the natural history of Ha Long Bay. Each cave has its own unique features, and visitors are often amazed by the beauty and mystery of these underground worlds.

• **The Legends of Ha Long Bay**

Ha Long Bay is not only known for its stunning scenery but also for the many legends that surround it. The name Ha Long means "Descending Dragon," and according to legend, the bay was created by dragons sent by the gods to help protect Vietnam from invaders. The dragons, breathing fire and spitting jewels, created the islands and rocks of the bay to form a natural barrier against enemy ships. After the battle was won, the dragons descended into the bay, where they remain to this day.

This legend adds a sense of magic and mystery to Ha Long Bay, and many visitors are drawn to the area not just for its beauty, but for the stories that have been passed down through generations. The myths and legends of Ha Long Bay are often shared by local guides, adding a cultural layer to the experience of visiting this natural wonder.

Ho Chi Minh City (Saigon)

Ho Chi Minh City, still often referred to as Saigon, is Vietnam's largest city and a bustling metropolis that blends modern skyscrapers with historic landmarks. This energetic city is a place where the past and present come together, offering visitors a rich cultural experience. From exploring historical sites like the War Remnants Museum and Notre-Dame Cathedral to immersing yourself in the city's vibrant street life, there's much to see and do in Ho Chi Minh City.

• War Remnants Museum

The War Remnants Museum is one of the most visited landmarks in Ho Chi Minh City, offering a sobering look at the Vietnam

War from a Vietnamese perspective. Originally known as the Exhibition House for US and Puppet Crimes, the museum's exhibits focus on the effects of the war, particularly the devastation caused by bombings, Agent Orange, and other weapons.

Inside the museum, visitors will find a collection of photographs, documents, and military equipment that tell the story of the war. Some of the most impactful exhibits include graphic photos of the war's impact on civilians, personal accounts from survivors, and artifacts such as tanks, planes, and helicopters that were used during the conflict. While the exhibits can be emotionally challenging, they provide important insights into the war and its lasting effects on Vietnam.

Outside the museum, there are also larger displays, including military tanks and aircraft used by both the U.S. and Vietnamese forces. The War Remnants Museum serves as a reminder of the struggles faced during the war and the resilience of the Vietnamese people. It's a must-visit for anyone wanting to better understand the country's history.

• Notre-Dame Cathedral

Not far from the War Remnants Museum is the Notre-Dame Cathedral, an iconic symbol of Saigon's colonial past. Built between 1877 and 1883 by French colonists, this beautiful church stands in the heart of the city. The cathedral's twin bell towers, rising nearly 60 meters, are one of the most recognizable landmarks in Ho Chi Minh City.

The Notre-Dame Cathedral is made entirely of materials imported from France, including the red bricks used for the exterior, which have retained their original color despite the passage of time. The architecture combines Gothic and Romanesque styles, with stunning stained-glass windows and intricate carvings.

While the church is still an active place of worship, it is also a popular spot for tourists. Visitors can step inside the cathedral to admire its vaulted ceilings and peaceful atmosphere, offering a contrast to the bustling city streets outside.

On weekends, the area around the cathedral fills with locals and tourists alike, making it a lively part of the city's cultural scene.

Next to the cathedral is another historical building, the Saigon Central Post Office, which was also designed by French architects. With its grand arches and classic design, it adds to the French colonial charm of this part of the city.

• **Vibrant Street Life**

One of the defining features of Ho Chi Minh City is its vibrant street life. The city's streets are always bustling with activity, from the roar of motorbikes weaving through traffic to the lively sounds of street vendors selling everything from fresh fruit to traditional Vietnamese street food.

A walk through the city's streets will lead you to some of the most colorful markets, where locals shop for fresh produce, clothing, and household goods. One of the most famous markets in Ho Chi Minh City is the Ben Thanh Market, which is located in the city center. Here, you can browse through hundreds of stalls selling a wide variety of items, including souvenirs, handicrafts, and clothing. The market is also a great place to sample local Vietnamese dishes, such as pho (noodle soup), banh mi (Vietnamese sandwich), and spring rolls.

The street food scene in Ho Chi Minh City is legendary. Small food carts line the streets, offering everything from grilled meat skewers to bowls of noodles and fresh fruit juices. Sampling the street food is a must for any visitor looking to experience the authentic flavors of Vietnamese cuisine. Some popular dishes to try include banh xeo (crispy Vietnamese pancake), goi cuon (fresh spring rolls), and the city's famous Vietnamese iced coffee, served with sweetened condensed milk.

Beyond the markets and street food, the streets of Saigon are also known for their lively nightlife. As the sun sets, the city's bars and restaurants come to life, offering everything from craft beer to rooftop views of the city skyline. The Bui Vien Street in the Backpacker District is one of the most energetic places to visit in the evening, with its neon lights, music, and crowds of people enjoying the nightlife.

• **Blend of Old and New**

Ho Chi Minh City is a place where the old and new exist side by side. In addition to the historical landmarks, the city is home to modern skyscrapers, luxury hotels, and shopping malls. The Bitexco Financial Tower, one of the tallest buildings in Vietnam, offers panoramic views of the city from its skydeck, giving visitors a bird's-eye view of the bustling streets below.

While the city has embraced modernization, it has also held on to its rich cultural traditions. Pagodas and temples can still be found throughout the city, offering a quiet escape from the busy streets. The Jade Emperor Pagoda, for example, is a popular spot for both locals and tourists who come to offer prayers and admire its beautiful architecture.

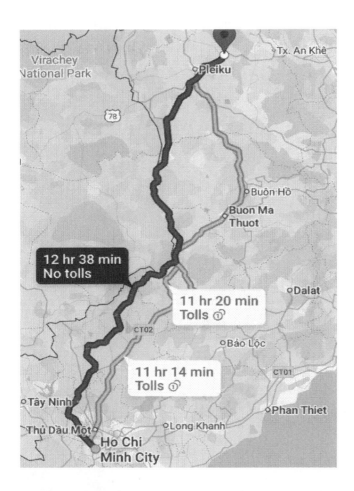

• The map above shows distance (with time covered) from Vietnam central area to Ho Chi Minh city

Hoi An

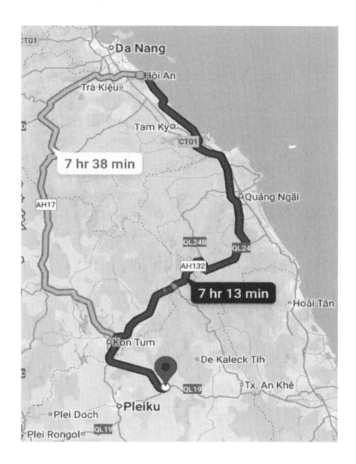

- The map above shows distance (with time covered) from Vietnam central area to Hoi An

Hoi An, a charming town located along Vietnam's central coast, is one of the country's most picturesque and well-preserved historic cities. Known for its lantern-lit streets, traditional crafts, and proximity to beautiful beaches, Hoi An offers visitors a unique blend of cultural heritage and natural beauty. Its ancient town, recognized as a UNESCO World Heritage Site, has made it a favorite destination for travelers seeking a glimpse into Vietnam's past while enjoying the tranquility of its serene streets and coastline.

• Lantern-Lit Streets

One of the most enchanting aspects of Hoi An is its nightly transformation into a city of light. As the sun sets, the streets of the Ancient Town come alive with thousands of colorful silk lanterns, creating a warm and magical atmosphere. These lanterns hang from trees, shops, and bridges, giving Hoi An its distinctive, romantic ambiance.

The Hoi An Lantern Festival, which takes place every month on the night of the full moon, is a particularly special time to visit. During the festival, the streets are closed to motorized traffic, and the town becomes illuminated solely by the soft glow of lanterns. Locals and tourists alike release floating lanterns into the Thu Bon River, making a wish as they watch the delicate lights drift across the water. The sight of the lanterns reflecting off the river's surface is a breathtaking moment that captures the spirit of Hoi An.

Even outside of the festival, visitors can stroll through the lantern-lit streets, visit local shops selling handmade lanterns, and enjoy the peaceful atmosphere that makes Hoi An so unique. Walking through the narrow alleys, you'll discover small, family-run shops selling silk clothing, handicrafts, and traditional artwork.

• **Traditional Crafts**

Hoi An has a rich history as a trading port, and many of its traditional crafts have been passed down through generations. The town is famous for its tailoring, with numerous tailor shops offering custom-made clothing that can be crafted and fitted within a day or two. Visitors can choose from a wide selection of fabrics and styles, making it easy to bring home a one-of-a-kind piece of Vietnamese fashion.

Another popular craft in Hoi An is silk weaving. The town's silk shops and workshops offer visitors the chance to see how silk is produced, from the silkworms to the final product. Hoi An's silk is known for its high quality, and you'll find beautiful scarves, dresses, and home décor items made from this luxurious material.

In addition to tailoring and silk, Hoi An is also known for its pottery. A short trip from the town center brings you to the Thanh Ha Pottery Village, where artisans create delicate ceramics using traditional methods. Visitors can try their hand at making their own pottery, offering a fun and hands-on way to engage with Hoi An's cultural heritage.

If you're interested in seeing how Hoi An's iconic lanterns are made, a visit to one of the lantern-making workshops is a must. Here, you can learn the process of crafting these colorful creations and even make your own lantern to take home as a souvenir.

• **Beaches**

While Hoi An's ancient streets are the town's most famous attraction, it's also home to some beautiful beaches that offer a relaxing escape from the hustle and bustle of the town center. Just a short bike or taxi ride away are An Bang Beach and Cua Dai Beach, two of the most popular coastal spots in the area.

An Bang Beach is known for its laid-back atmosphere, soft white sand, and clear blue waters. It's the perfect place to unwind, swim, or enjoy a drink at one of the beachfront cafes. The beach is lined with palm trees, offering plenty of shaded spots to relax, and it's a favorite destination for both locals and tourists.

Cua Dai Beach, located slightly farther from the town, offers a more secluded setting with fewer crowds. The beach is an excellent spot for sunbathing, swimming, and taking in the natural beauty of the coastline. Although erosion has affected parts of the beach, it still remains a popular choice for visitors looking for a peaceful day by the sea.

For those who enjoy water sports, both beaches offer opportunities for activities like paddleboarding, kayaking, and surfing. Renting a bike and cycling from the town to the beach is also a popular activity, allowing visitors to take in the scenic countryside along the way.

• The Blend of Cultures in Hoi An

Hoi An's rich history as a trading port has shaped its cultural diversity. The town was once an important stop for merchants from Japan, China, and Europe, and this influence can still be seen today in its architecture and cuisine. The Japanese Covered Bridge, an iconic symbol of Hoi An, reflects the town's historical connections with Japan, while the Chinese Assembly Halls showcase the influence of Chinese merchants.

Walking through the ancient town, you'll see a blend of these cultures in the design of the buildings, which include Chinese-style pagodas, French colonial houses, and traditional wooden Vietnamese shops. The mix of cultural influences gives Hoi An a unique character that sets it apart from other destinations in Vietnam.

Hoi An's food is also a reflection of its multicultural past. Some of the must-try dishes include cao lầu, a noodle dish that is said to be influenced by Japanese soba noodles, and white rose dumplings, a local specialty with Chinese roots. The town's street food scene is vibrant, with stalls offering everything from banh mi sandwiches to fresh seafood dishes. Taking a cooking class is a popular activity in Hoi An, where visitors can learn to make traditional Vietnamese dishes using fresh, local ingredients.

Hue

Hue, located in central Vietnam along the banks of the Perfume River, is a city that holds great historical significance. As the former capital of the Nguyen Dynasty, Hue is home to some of Vietnam's most important cultural and architectural treasures, including the Imperial Citadel, ancient pagodas, and royal tombs. These landmarks offer visitors a fascinating glimpse into the country's royal past, while the city itself maintains a tranquil, laid-back charm that contrasts with the hustle of other Vietnamese cities.

• **The Imperial Citadel**

At the heart of Hue lies the Imperial Citadel, a vast complex that once served as the political, cultural, and religious center of the Nguyen Dynasty. Built in the early 19th century, this UNESCO World Heritage Site was inspired by the Forbidden City in Beijing, with high walls, imposing gates, and intricate buildings designed to impress and protect the royal family.

The citadel is divided into different sections, with the Purple Forbidden City at its core. This area was once reserved for the emperor and his closest family members and is where many important ceremonies and events took place. Although parts of the citadel were damaged during wars, ongoing restoration efforts have brought much of its former glory back to life.

As you walk through the imposing Ngo Mon Gate—the main entrance to the citadel—you'll be greeted by grand courtyards, halls, and palaces that reflect the grandeur of Vietnam's imperial era. Key highlights include the Thai Hoa Palace, where emperors would hold court, and the Truong Sanh Residence, which was once the home of royal family members. The citadel's architecture features a blend of traditional Vietnamese design with influences from Chinese and French styles, showcasing the cultural exchange that occurred during the Nguyen Dynasty's rule.

For history enthusiasts, a visit to the Hue Museum of Royal Fine Arts inside the citadel is a must. The museum displays a wide range of artifacts from the Nguyen Dynasty, including royal costumes, ceramics, and decorative items that offer insight into the lavish lifestyle of the royal family.

• Ancient Pagodas

Hue is also known for its ancient pagodas, which provide a peaceful and spiritual retreat from the city's historical landmarks. The most famous of these is the Thien Mu Pagoda, located on a hill overlooking the Perfume River. This seven-story pagoda is the tallest in Vietnam and is considered a symbol of Hue.

The Thien Mu Pagoda has a rich history, dating back to the 17th century, and is closely tied to Vietnamese Buddhism. As you explore the pagoda, you'll find beautiful statues, tranquil gardens, and ancient relics that reflect its religious significance. The views from the pagoda are also breathtaking, offering a panoramic look over the river and surrounding countryside.

Another important religious site is the Tu Dam Pagoda, one of the most active Buddhist temples in Hue. This pagoda is known for its peaceful atmosphere, with monks often chanting prayers in the early morning and late afternoon. Visitors are welcome to observe or participate in the rituals, providing a deeper connection to the spiritual traditions of Vietnam.

Hue's pagodas are not only places of worship but also important historical and cultural landmarks that have played a key role in the city's religious and political life over the centuries.

• Royal Tombs

Scattered across the countryside around Hue are the royal tombs of the Nguyen emperors, each a unique reflection of the ruler it was built to honor. These tombs are grand, intricately designed complexes that blend traditional Vietnamese architecture with natural landscapes, often set against the backdrop of rivers, mountains, or forests.

One of the most impressive royal tombs is the Tomb of Emperor Tu Duc, who ruled from 1847 to 1883. This tomb, located in a tranquil forested area, is both a resting place and a retreat where the emperor would spend time during his life. The complex includes palaces, temples, and pavilions, all set around a peaceful lake. Visitors can wander through the beautifully landscaped grounds and explore the various structures, gaining insight into the emperor's personal life and reign.

Another notable site is the Tomb of Emperor Khai Dinh, known for its striking blend of Vietnamese and European architectural styles. Built in the early 20th century, this tomb is more modern than others and stands out for its intricate mosaic decorations, which combine traditional dragon motifs with modern elements like glass and ceramics. The tomb's interior is particularly impressive, with walls and ceilings adorned with detailed frescoes and carvings that reflect Khai Dinh's eclectic tastes.

The Tomb of Minh Mang, located near the Perfume River, is another must-visit. This tomb is renowned for its harmonious design, where buildings are carefully integrated into the natural landscape. The symmetry of the layout and the serene surroundings make it a peaceful and contemplative place to visit.

Exploring the royal tombs offers a deeper understanding of the personal lives of Vietnam's emperors and the cultural and artistic achievements of the Nguyen Dynasty. Each tomb is a work of art in its own right, reflecting the personality, beliefs, and reign of the emperor it commemorates.

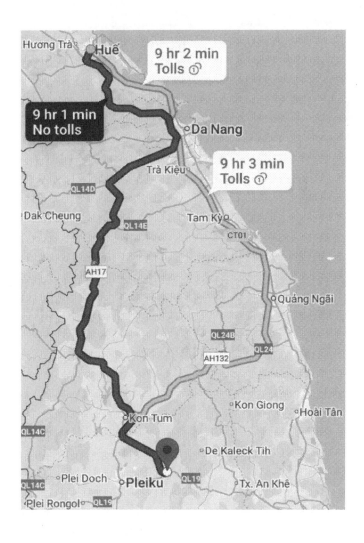

- **The map above shows distance (with time covered) from Vietnam central area to Hue**

Insider travel tips for Vietnam

Traveling through Vietnam is an adventure that offers both modern conveniences and a deep connection to history. Whether you're navigating the bustling streets of Ho Chi Minh City or enjoying the peaceful countryside in Hoi An, knowing a few insider travel tips can make your trip more enjoyable and immersive.

• Transportation

Vietnam has a well-developed transportation network, making it relatively easy to get from one place to another, but understanding your options can help you travel more smoothly.

1. Flights

For long-distance travel between major cities like Hanoi, Ho Chi Minh City, and Da Nang, domestic flights are the fastest and most convenient option. Airlines like Vietnam Airlines, VietJet Air, and Bamboo Airways offer regular flights at affordable prices. Booking flights in advance can help secure lower fares, especially during the peak travel seasons.

2. Trains

Vietnam's Reunification Express train runs from Hanoi to Ho Chi Minh City, offering a scenic and affordable way to see the country. The journey is long (around 30-35 hours), but for shorter trips, such as Hanoi to Hue or Da Nang, the train is a comfortable option. There are different classes, ranging from hard seats to soft sleepers, depending on your budget and comfort level.

3. Buses

Long-distance buses are another affordable option, with services connecting most cities and towns. Sleeper buses are particularly common for overnight journeys. Be prepared for local quirks like unpredictable schedules and varying comfort levels. While buses are cheap, travelers should watch out for safety and comfort, especially on overnight routes.

4. Motorbikes

For those seeking more independence and adventure, motorbikes are a popular way to explore Vietnam. Renting a motorbike allows you to travel at your own pace and visit off-the-beaten-path locations.

It's important to have experience riding motorbikes and to familiarize yourself with local traffic laws, which can be chaotic.

In cities, ride-hailing apps like Grab offer motorbike taxis, which are a quick and affordable way to get around.

5. Taxis and Ride-hailing

Taxis are plentiful in big cities, but it's important to use reputable companies like Mai Linh or Vinasun to avoid overcharging.

For convenience, ride-hailing apps like Grab and Gojek (available in some areas) are widely used, offering both car and motorbike services.

6. Cycling and Walking

In smaller towns like Hoi An, renting a bicycle is a great way to explore.

Many areas are bike-friendly, and it's a relaxing way to visit local markets, beaches, and countryside villages.

Walking is also a wonderful way to experience cities like Hanoi, where narrow alleys and busy streets offer an up-close look at local life.

• **Cuisine**

Vietnamese cuisine is one of the highlights of any trip, with its bold flavors, fresh ingredients, and regional diversity. Here are some must-try dishes and tips to enjoy the food scene.

1. Pho

Vietnam's most famous dish, pho, is a noodle soup made with beef or chicken, herbs, and a flavorful broth. While you can find pho throughout the country, the recipe can vary between regions. Hanoi is known for its lighter, more traditional version, while the southern version in Ho Chi Minh City tends to be sweeter and more flavorful.

2. Banh Mi

A delicious fusion of French and Vietnamese cuisine, banh mi is a sandwich made with a crispy baguette filled with meats like pork or chicken, pickled vegetables, cilantro, and a dash of chili. It's a popular street food that you can find everywhere, from small roadside stalls to cafes.

3. Bun Cha

Particularly famous in Hanoi, bun cha consists of grilled pork served with rice noodles, fresh herbs, and a dipping sauce made from fish sauce, lime, and sugar. It's a simple yet flavorful dish that's loved by locals and visitors alike.

4. Cao Lau

A specialty of Hoi An, cao lau is a noodle dish made with thick, chewy noodles, pork, fresh herbs, and crispy croutons. It's said that the dish's unique flavor comes from the water drawn from ancient wells in the region.

5. Seafood

Vietnam's coastal areas, such as Ha Long Bay and Nha Trang, are famous for their fresh seafood. Look for dishes like grilled squid, steamed fish, and clams in lemongrass. Visiting a seafood restaurant by the sea ensures the freshest catch, and you can often pick your seafood directly from tanks.

6. Local Markets

Eating at local markets is one of the best ways to experience authentic Vietnamese food. Markets like Ben Thanh Market in Ho Chi Minh City or the Dong Xuan Market in Hanoi offer a variety of street food stalls serving everything from spring rolls to sticky rice.

Don't be afraid to try new things—Vietnamese street food is both affordable and delicious.

• Local Experiences

To get the most out of your trip to Vietnam, take time to engage with the local culture and traditions.

1. Street Life

Vietnam's cities, especially Hanoi and Ho Chi Minh City, are known for their vibrant street life. From morning markets to evening street food stalls, life happens on the sidewalks. Spend time walking around the Old Quarter in Hanoi or the Ben Thanh Market in Ho Chi Minh City to see the daily rhythm of life in Vietnam.

2. Local Festivals

If you visit Vietnam during the Tet Festival (Lunar New Year), you'll experience the country's most important celebration. Families gather, streets are decorated with flowers, and special foods are prepared. It's a time for reunions and honoring ancestors, and if you're lucky enough to be invited into a local's home, it's a special experience.

3. Traditional Crafts

Many regions in Vietnam are known for their traditional crafts, and visiting local artisans is a great way to learn about the country's cultural heritage. In Hoi An, for example, you can watch local craftsmen making lanterns, pottery, or tailored clothing. You can also visit Bat Trang village near Hanoi to see traditional ceramics being made.

4. Homestays

For a more personal experience, consider staying in a homestay in the countryside. Many rural areas, such as Sapa or the Mekong Delta, offer opportunities to stay with local families, where you can enjoy home-cooked meals and learn about the local way of life.

Chapter Three: Cambodia

Phnom Penh

Phnom Penh, the capital of Cambodia, is a city where both beauty and deep historical reflection come together. While it serves as a gateway to Cambodia's past and present, Phnom Penh's rich culture and harrowing history make it a powerful destination for visitors. Some of the city's key landmarks include the Royal Palace, the Silver Pagoda, and historical sites tied to the Khmer Rouge regime, such as the Killing Fields and the Tuol Sleng Genocide Museum.

• Royal Palace

The Royal Palace is one of Phnom Penh's most iconic landmarks, representing the Cambodian monarchy and a long history of Khmer architecture. Built in the 19th century, it serves as the official residence of the King of Cambodia. The palace's golden spires rise above the city, showcasing traditional Khmer architectural styles.

Visitors can explore several parts of the palace grounds, including the Throne Hall, where royal ceremonies take place. The hall's interior is adorned with intricate decorations and gilded furnishings, reflecting the grandeur of Cambodian royalty. The palace gardens are beautifully maintained, offering a peaceful space to walk and appreciate the traditional Khmer landscaping.

• **Silver Pagoda**

Located within the Royal Palace complex is the Silver Pagoda, named for the gleaming silver tiles that cover its floor. This sacred temple, also known as Wat Preah Keo, houses many important religious artifacts, including a life-sized gold Buddha encrusted with diamonds and a revered Emerald Buddha made of baccarat crystal.

The Silver Pagoda is a place of worship and pilgrimage for Cambodians, making it not only a stunning piece of architecture but also a spiritual hub. Visitors are invited to respectfully explore the temple and its treasures, getting a glimpse into the deeply rooted Buddhist traditions of Cambodia.

• **Killing Fields**

One of the most sobering sites in Phnom Penh is the Killing Fields of Choeung Ek. Located about 15 kilometers from the city, the Killing Fields are a mass grave site where tens of thousands of Cambodians were executed by the Khmer Rouge regime between 1975 and 1979. This period, under the leadership of Pol Pot, was one of the darkest chapters in Cambodia's history.

The Choeung Ek Memorial, marked by a towering stupa filled with the skulls of victims, stands as a reminder of the horrors of the genocide. Visitors can walk through the grounds, which include mass graves and chilling reminders of the atrocities that took place there. Audio guides provide firsthand accounts of survivors and detailed information about the genocide, making it a powerful place for reflection and remembrance.

• Tuol Sleng Genocide Museum

Equally poignant is the Tuol Sleng Genocide Museum, a former high school that was turned into a prison and torture facility known as S-21 by the Khmer Rouge. Thousands of men, women, and children were detained, tortured, and later executed after being brought to this prison during Pol Pot's regime.

The museum provides an in-depth look at the horrors faced by those imprisoned here. Photos of victims, prison cells, and torture devices are on display, along with accounts from survivors. Although a difficult place to visit, Tuol Sleng is essential for understanding Cambodia's recent history and the resilience of its people.

• **Phnom Penh's Contrasts**

While Phnom Penh's history can be emotionally heavy, the city is also vibrant and full of life. Today, Phnom Penh is experiencing rapid development, with modern cafes, bustling markets, and lively riverside promenades juxtaposing the more somber historical landmarks. The Phsar Thmey (Central Market) and Russian Market are great spots for shopping, where you can find everything from souvenirs to local delicacies.

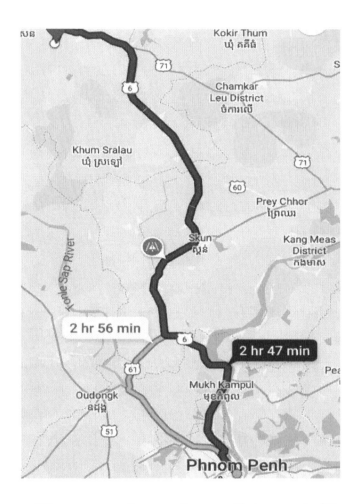

• The map above shows distance (with time covered) from Cambodia central area to Phnom Penh

Siem Reap

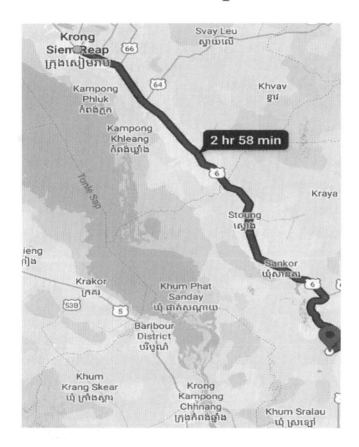

- The map above shows distance (with time covered) from Cambodia central area to Siem Reap

Siem Reap, located in northwestern Cambodia, is world-renowned as the gateway to one of the most breathtaking archaeological wonders, Angkor Wat. This small city, once a quiet village, has grown into a vibrant hub for travelers eager to explore the vast Angkor temple complex and experience the charm of Cambodian culture. The main draw, of course, is Angkor Wat itself—an iconic symbol of Cambodia, rich in history and architectural marvels.

• **Angkor Wat**

Angkor Wat, the largest religious monument in the world, is the crown jewel of the Angkor Archaeological Park. Built in the early 12th century by King Suryavarman II, it was originally dedicated to the Hindu god Vishnu before later becoming a Buddhist temple. The temple's intricate carvings, massive galleries, and towering spires are a testament to the brilliance of Khmer architecture.

The central towers of Angkor Wat are shaped like lotus buds, and the walls are covered with thousands of detailed bas-reliefs, depicting stories from Hindu mythology, scenes of battle, and daily life in the Khmer empire. As you explore, you'll find courtyards, walkways, and libraries that all reveal a glimpse into the life and culture of the time.

Visitors often spend hours wandering the halls, marveling at the craftsmanship that has withstood centuries. Though Angkor Wat is the most famous of the temples, it is only one of many remarkable structures in the Angkor complex.

• Sunrise at Angkor Wat

One of the most unforgettable experiences in Siem Reap is witnessing the sunrise at

Angkor Wat. As the first light of the day illuminates the sky, the temple is reflected in the still waters of the surrounding moat, creating a truly mesmerizing scene. The soft glow of the sun slowly reveals the silhouette of the temple's spires, making it a moment of serenity and beauty.

Many visitors choose to arrive at the temple before dawn to secure the best spot for viewing. The sight of the sun rising behind this ancient structure is a photographer's dream, and even for those not inclined to take photos, it is a spiritual and awe-inspiring experience.

• Exploring Other Temples

While Angkor Wat is the centerpiece, the Angkor complex is home to hundreds of temples, each with its unique history and design. Angkor Thom is a notable place. It's the last capital of the Khmer empire and a great site worth paying a visit.

Within Angkor Thom lies the Bayon Temple, famous for its giant stone faces that smile enigmatically from its towers. These faces, believed to represent the Bodhisattva Avalokiteshvara or the King himself, create an eerie yet captivating atmosphere.

Not far from Angkor Wat is Ta Prohm, also known as the "Tomb Raider Temple" due to its appearance in the film. Ta Prohm is famous for the way nature has intertwined with its structures.

Massive trees grow over and through the temple walls, their roots snaking around the stone, creating a surreal and mysterious scene.

• Siem Reap's Cultural Offerings

Beyond the temples, Siem Reap offers plenty of other activities to help you immerse yourself in Cambodian culture.

Phare, the Cambodian Circus, is a unique blend of theater, acrobatics, and traditional storytelling, showcasing the talent and resilience of young Cambodians.

Visitors can also explore the Angkor National Museum, which houses ancient artifacts from the Khmer Empire and provides context to the grandeur of the temples.

Siem Reap's Old Market (Psar Chas) and Pub Street are lively areas where travelers can shop for local crafts and taste traditional Cambodian dishes like amok (a fragrant coconut milk curry).

• **Practical Tips for Visiting the Angkor Complex**

- Ticketing

The Angkor Archaeological Park requires an entrance pass, available as a 1-day, 3-day, or 7-day ticket.

If you plan to visit several temples, the multi-day passes are highly recommended.

- Transportation

To explore the sprawling complex, many visitors hire a tuk-tuk driver for the day or rent bicycles to navigate the temple grounds at their own pace.

- What to Wear

Angkor Wat and the surrounding temples are religious sites, so it's important to dress modestly.

- Timing

Early morning and late afternoon are the best times to visit, not only for cooler temperatures but also to avoid the crowds that tend to arrive later in the day.

Sihanoukville

Sihanoukville, located on the southwestern coast of Cambodia, is the country's top destination for beach lovers. Known for its tropical beaches, turquoise waters, and a relaxed atmosphere, this coastal town offers the perfect escape from the hustle and bustle of Cambodia's major cities. Whether you're looking to unwind on the sand, explore nearby islands, or enjoy fresh seafood by the sea, Sihanoukville has something for every traveler seeking coastal relaxation.

• Sihanoukville's Beaches

Sihanoukville's beaches are its main attraction. The town is home to several beautiful stretches of sand, each with its unique vibe and character. Otres Beach is one of the most popular, offering a laid-back atmosphere with soft white sand, swaying palm trees, and calm waters perfect for swimming. It's a great spot for sunbathing, reading a book under a beach umbrella, or taking a peaceful stroll along the shoreline.

For those seeking a more lively beach scene, Serendipity Beach is known for its beach bars, guesthouses, and a vibrant nightlife. Here, you can enjoy a cocktail as you watch the sunset, followed by a fresh seafood barbecue in the evening. The lively atmosphere makes Serendipity Beach a favorite for younger travelers looking for a fun time by the sea.

Independence Beach is a quieter alternative, ideal for families or anyone wanting a more peaceful environment. The shallow waters are safe for children, and the beach's wide expanse provides plenty of space for everyone to spread out and enjoy the sun.

• Island Escapes

Just off the coast of Sihanoukville lie some of Cambodia's most stunning islands, offering a true tropical getaway. Koh Rong, the largest of the islands, is famous for its powdery white sand beaches, crystal-clear waters, and vibrant marine life. The island is a haven for those looking to experience a mix of adventure and relaxation. You can snorkel or dive to explore the coral reefs, hike through the jungle, or simply lounge on the beach, soaking in the tranquility.

For an even quieter escape, Koh Rong Samloem is a smaller island known for its peaceful and undeveloped charm. With fewer tourists, it offers a more serene experience. The island's Saracen Bay is a stretch of untouched beach that feels like a secluded paradise, perfect for couples or solo travelers looking to disconnect from the outside world. Many visitors spend their days here swimming, kayaking, or just relaxing in the shade of palm trees.

Both Koh Rong and Koh Rong Samloem can be easily reached by ferry from Sihanoukville, making them ideal day trips or overnight stays for those wanting to explore beyond the mainland.

• **Coastal Relaxation and Local Seafood**

One of the best ways to experience Sihanoukville is by indulging in the local seafood, which is both fresh and affordable. The town's many beachside restaurants serve up delicious dishes, such as grilled prawns, squid, and crab, often cooked with local herbs and spices. Dining with your feet in the sand as the waves lap at the shore is a must-try experience.

For a more local experience, the Sihanoukville Fishing Port is where you can see fishermen bring in their catch of the day. You can even buy fresh seafood here and have it prepared at a nearby restaurant for a truly authentic meal.

• **Exploring Sihanoukville's Natural Beauty**

Beyond the beaches, Sihanoukville is also home to natural attractions worth exploring. Ream National Park, located just outside of the city, offers visitors the chance to experience Cambodia's coastal wetlands and mangrove forests. The park is a haven for birdwatchers and nature lovers, with opportunities to spot a variety of wildlife, including dolphins in the waters just off the coast.

For those interested in more active pursuits, kayaking through the park's mangroves or hiking its forest trails are great ways to explore the area's natural beauty. The park also offers boat tours that take you along the coast, where you can visit hidden beaches and enjoy the scenery.

• Practical Tips for Visiting Sihanoukville

- Getting There

Sihanoukville is well-connected by bus from Phnom Penh and other parts of Cambodia. There is also an international airport with flights from nearby countries.

- Transportation

Tuk-tuks and motorbikes are common ways to get around Sihanoukville. They're affordable and allow you to explore the different beaches and areas at your own pace.

- Where to Stay

Accommodations range from budget-friendly beach bungalows to upscale resorts, particularly around Otres Beach and the islands. Whether you're a backpacker or seeking luxury, there's something for every budget.

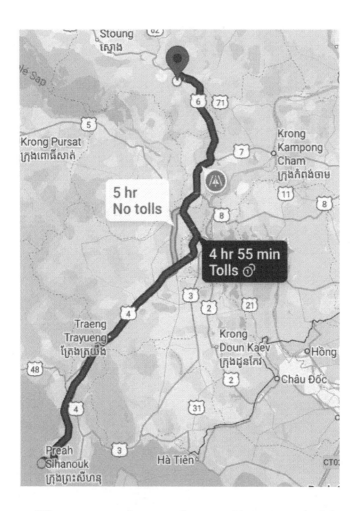

• The map above shows distance (with time covered) from Cambodia central area to Sihanoukville

Battambang

Battambang, located in northwestern Cambodia, is a city known for its well-preserved French colonial architecture, charming countryside, and unique experiences like the famous bamboo train. Although it's not as widely visited as Siem Reap or Phnom Penh, Battambang offers a more laid-back and authentic Cambodian experience. It's the perfect destination for travelers interested in history, culture, and rural life.

• French Colonial Heritage

Battambang's history is deeply intertwined with its time as part of French Indochina in the late 19th and early 20th centuries. The city's downtown area still features many buildings from the colonial era, which gives Battambang a distinctive European feel. The well-preserved French colonial architecture is a highlight, with old shophouses, administrative buildings, and villas lining the streets. A stroll through the city center feels like stepping back in time, offering a glimpse of Cambodia's past.

One of the most iconic buildings is the Battambang Governor's Residence, a grand structure that showcases the elegance of colonial design.

Other notable landmarks include the Central Market and the Wat Damrey Sor, a temple with French influences. Exploring these sites provides a fascinating look at how European and local styles merged to create Battambang's unique architectural identity.

• **The Bamboo Train**

Battambang is famous for its quirky and fun attraction: the Norry, or bamboo train. This makeshift railway system is unlike any train you've ever been on. It consists of a simple bamboo platform mounted on wheels, powered by a small engine. Originally used to transport goods and locals through the countryside, the bamboo train has now become a popular activity for tourists.

Riding the bamboo train offers a thrilling, bumpy ride through the Cambodian countryside. As the train zips along the tracks at surprising speeds, you'll pass rice fields, small villages, and scenic landscapes.

Since the tracks are single-line, it's common to encounter oncoming trains, at which point one of the trains is disassembled to let the other pass. It's a fun and interactive experience that showcases the ingenuity of local transportation.

While the original bamboo train was closed for some time, a new track has been built outside the city, continuing the tradition for visitors to enjoy this unique ride.

• **Countryside Tours**

One of the best reasons to visit Battambang is to explore the beautiful countryside that surrounds the city. The rural areas around Battambang are known for their fertile lands, rice paddies, and traditional villages. Guided countryside tours are a great way to experience local life, meet farmers, and learn about Cambodia's agricultural practices.

You can visit Phnom Banan, an ancient hilltop temple that offers stunning views of the surrounding landscape. The climb to the top is worth it, not just for the views, but also for the chance to explore this lesser-known historical site. The temple is much quieter than the famous Angkor Wat, allowing for a peaceful and reflective experience.

Another interesting stop is the Killing Caves of Phnom Sampeau, a somber but important historical site. During the Khmer Rouge regime, these caves were used as execution sites, and today they stand as a reminder of Cambodia's tragic past. Visitors can pay their respects at the memorials and take in the panoramic views from the top of the mountain.

For a more lighthearted experience, don't miss the Bat Cave, located near Phnom Sampeau. Every evening at sunset, thousands of bats stream out of the cave in a mesmerizing display, heading out to forage for food. It's a fascinating natural spectacle that draws many visitors.

• Local Arts and Culture

Battambang is also a hub for Cambodia's growing arts scene. The city has a number of art galleries and cultural centers, showcasing works from local artists. Phare Ponleu Selpak, a renowned local organization, is dedicated to promoting Cambodian arts and supporting at-risk youth. They offer circus performances that combine traditional and modern arts, providing a glimpse into the creativity and resilience of the local community.

Visiting these cultural centers is a great way to support local artists while gaining a deeper understanding of Cambodia's contemporary culture and art forms.

• **Practical Tips for Visiting Battambang**

- Getting There

Battambang is easily accessible by bus from both Phnom Penh and Siem Reap. The journey offers scenic views of the countryside and takes about 4-5 hours from either city. You can also travel by boat from Siem Reap, a scenic but longer option that lets you experience life along the Tonle Sap River.

- Transportation

The city itself is best explored by tuk-tuk, and hiring a local driver for the day is an affordable way to see both the city's main sights and the surrounding countryside. Many countryside tours are available, and tuk-tuk drivers can also guide you to the best spots.

- Where to Stay

Battambang has a variety of accommodation options, ranging from budget guesthouses to mid-range hotels. The city's laid-back vibe makes it a great place to relax and unwind, and many guesthouses offer free bicycles for guests to explore the town at their own pace.

Insider travel tips for Cambodia

To make the most of your trip, it's helpful to understand some key customs, language basics, and the best ways to enjoy the local food. These tips will not only help you navigate Cambodia more comfortably but also ensure you connect more deeply with the people and culture.

• **Customs and Etiquette**

Cambodia has a rich cultural heritage influenced by its Buddhist beliefs, and it's important to be aware of local customs to show respect during your visit. Here are some things to keep in mind:

1. Greeting and Respect

The traditional Cambodian greeting is called the "Sampeah," where you place your palms together in front of your chest and bow slightly. The higher your hands are positioned, the more respect you show. Cambodians usually greet elders or monks with a higher sampeah than friends or peers.

2. Monks and Temples

Monks hold a special place in Cambodian society, and you'll see them in many cities and temples. Be respectful when interacting with monks. Women should avoid touching monks or handing items directly to them.

3. Modesty

Cambodians tend to dress conservatively, especially in rural areas and religious sites. Wearing revealing clothing might be considered disrespectful. If you're visiting temples or sacred places, it's best to wear long sleeves and pants or a long skirt.

4. Public Displays of Affection

Cambodians are modest, and public displays of affection like hugging or kissing are uncommon and can make locals uncomfortable. Holding hands is usually fine, but it's best to keep more affectionate gestures private.

5. Pointing and Gestures

Pointing with your finger is considered rude in Cambodia. Instead, gesture with your whole hand or use your thumb. Avoid touching people's heads, as the head is seen as the most sacred part of the body.

• **Language**

The official language of Cambodia is Khmer, and while many Cambodians, especially in tourist areas, speak some English, learning a few key phrases in Khmer can go a long way in making connections with locals. Here are some basic phrases that will be useful:

- **Hello:** _Suosdey_ (soo-oss-day)

- **Thank you:** _Orkun_ (aw-koon)

- **Yes:** _Baat_ (for men)/_Chaas_ (for women)

- **No:** _Ot teh_ (awt-tay)

- **How much?:** _Bon-man?_

- **Excuse me/Sorry:** _Som toh_ (sawm-toh)

Even though many people understand English, especially in larger cities like Phnom Penh and Siem Reap, using a few Khmer words can bring a smile to the faces of locals and create a warmer interaction.

• **Dining Experiences**

Cambodian cuisine is flavorful, diverse, and often very affordable. The food is a mix of influences from neighboring countries like Thailand and Vietnam, but it also has its own unique dishes that are worth trying.

Here's what you need to know to enjoy the local dining scene:

1. Popular Dishes to Try

- Amok Trey

This is one of Cambodia's most famous dishes, a fragrant curry made with fish, coconut milk, and Khmer spices, often served in a banana leaf bowl.

- Bai Sach Chrouk

A simple but delicious breakfast dish of grilled pork served over rice, often with a side of pickled vegetables.

- Lok Lak

Stir-fried beef served with rice, lettuce, tomatoes, and a dipping sauce made of lime juice and black pepper.

- Nom Banh Chok

This is a traditional Cambodian noodle dish, commonly eaten for breakfast. The noodles are served with a green curry sauce made from fish, lemongrass, turmeric, and kaffir lime.

2. Street Food

Cambodia has an abundance of street food stalls, especially in cities like Phnom Penh and Siem Reap. Popular street food items include skewers of grilled meats, spring rolls, fried noodles, and fresh fruit shakes.

Don't hesitate to try some local snacks, but always make sure the food looks fresh and is cooked thoroughly to avoid any stomach issues.

3. Dining Etiquette

- Chopsticks and Spoons

In Cambodia, rice-based meals are typically eaten with a spoon and fork, while noodle dishes are usually eaten with chopsticks.

When finished with your meal, avoid leaving chopsticks sticking upright in your bowl, as it is considered bad luck.

- Sharing Meals

Cambodian meals are often shared family-style, where several dishes are placed in the center of the table, and each person helps themselves. If you're invited to eat with locals, it's polite to try a little bit of everything.

- Drink with Ice

Cambodians often drink iced beverages, and while most restaurants and cafes use filtered ice, it's a good idea to check or ask about the water source if you're in more rural areas.

4. Vegetarian Options

Vegetarianism is not widespread in Cambodia, but many restaurants, especially in tourist areas, offer vegetarian versions of traditional dishes.

If you're in a smaller town or local eatery, it's helpful to know how to say "I don't eat meat" in Khmer: _Khnyom ot si saich_ (kn-yom ot see sigh).

• Transportation Tips

Getting around Cambodia can be an adventure, but with some preparation, it's fairly easy to navigate:

1. Tuk-tuks and Motorbikes

Tuk-tuks are one of the most popular ways to get around in Cambodian cities. They are affordable, and many drivers speak enough English to understand basic directions.

Always agree on a fare before getting in to avoid surprises. Motorbike taxis (motodops) are also common and are a faster way to get around, though they might be less comfortable.

2. Buses and Mini buses

If you're traveling between cities, buses are the most affordable and popular option. Long-distance buses run between major cities like Phnom Penh, Siem Reap, and Sihanoukville.

Some companies offer more comfortable buses with air conditioning and Wi-Fi.

3. Boats

For a more scenic journey, you can travel by boat along the Mekong River or the Tonle Sap River. Boats are slower than buses, but they offer beautiful views and a unique travel experience, especially the route between Phnom Penh and Siem Reap.

4. Renting Bicycles

In smaller cities like Battambang or Kampot, renting a bicycle is a great way to explore the area at your own pace. Many guesthouses and hotels offer bike rentals, and the slower pace allows you to see more of the countryside.

• Safety Considerations

Cambodia is generally safe for tourists, but as with any travel destination, there are a few things to keep in mind:

- Pickpocketing and Scams

In busy tourist areas, be aware of your belongings. Pickpocketing and bag snatching can happen, especially in crowded markets or near popular landmarks.

- Traffic

Traffic in Cambodian cities can be chaotic, and pedestrian crossings aren't always respected. When walking in cities, cross the road carefully and always keep an eye on motorbikes.

- Health Precautions

Make sure to stay hydrated, especially in the hot and humid months. Carry a refillable water bottle and drink bottled or filtered water.

It's also a good idea to have some basic medical supplies with you, as pharmacies in rural areas may not stock everything you need.

• Best Times to Visit

The weather in Cambodia varies throughout the year, with two main seasons: the dry season and the wet season.

- Dry Season (November to April)

This is the most popular time to visit Cambodia, especially from November to February when the temperatures are cooler. The weather is warm and dry, making it ideal for exploring temples, beaches, and the countryside.

- Wet Season (May to October)

The wet season is marked by heavy rain, but this doesn't mean you should avoid Cambodia. The rains usually come in short bursts, often in the afternoon, and the countryside is lush and green during this time. It's also the best time to visit the floating villages on Tonle Sap Lake, as the water levels are high.

Chapter Four: Laos

Luang Prabang

Luang Prabang is a serene and beautiful town in northern Laos, known for its peaceful atmosphere, rich history, and stunning natural beauty. As a UNESCO World Heritage Site, it offers a unique blend of traditional Laotian culture, colonial architecture, and breathtaking landscapes. It's a place where ancient temples, French colonial buildings, and the mighty Mekong River come together to create a timeless experience for visitors. From wandering through its quiet streets to exploring its lush surroundings, Luang Prabang is a place that leaves a lasting impression.

• UNESCO World Heritage Site

Luang Prabang's status as a UNESCO World Heritage Site is well-deserved. The town's unique mix of traditional Lao wooden houses and grand French colonial buildings makes it a living museum. As you walk through the streets, you'll see how the town's architecture reflects its history. The preservation of its cultural heritage is a key part of what makes Luang Prabang special. Many of the buildings are hundreds of years old, and efforts have been made to maintain their original beauty.

The heart of Luang Prabang is its connection to Buddhism, and this is reflected in the number of temples, or "wats", scattered throughout the town. There are more than 30 temples here, with monks in their saffron robes being a common sight. Wat Xieng Thong, one of the most important temples, is a must-visit. This temple, built in the 16th century, is known for its sweeping roofs and intricate mosaics. It is a symbol of the region's deep spiritual roots and architectural beauty.

• The Mekong River

The mighty Mekong River flows alongside Luang Prabang, adding to the town's tranquil vibe. The river is a lifeline for the people of Laos, providing water for farming and fishing.

It also offers visitors a chance to experience Luang Prabang from a different perspective. Taking a boat ride on the Mekong is a popular activity, allowing you to see the lush landscapes and rural villages along its banks.

One of the highlights is a sunset cruise on the river. As the sun sets over the hills, the water turns golden, creating a magical scene. Whether you're taking a slow boat to visit nearby attractions or simply enjoying a peaceful moment along the riverbank, the Mekong River is an essential part of the Luang Prabang experience.

• **Kuang Si Falls**

Just outside Luang Prabang, about 30 kilometers away, is Kuang Si Falls, one of the most beautiful natural attractions in Laos. The falls are a multi-tiered waterfall, with crystal-clear turquoise pools that invite visitors to swim and cool off.

The water flows down from the jungle into a series of limestone pools, making it look like something out of a fairy tale.

Visitors can enjoy hiking trails around the falls, offering stunning views of the cascading water. For those who love nature and adventure, a trip to Kuang Si Falls is a must.

There's also a bear rescue center near the falls, where you can learn about the work being done to protect endangered Asian black bears.

• **Traditional Temples**

In addition to Wat Xieng Thong, Luang Prabang is home to many other beautiful temples that reflect its deep spiritual history. One of these is Wat Mai, known for its golden bas-reliefs and five-tiered roof. This temple, located near the Royal Palace, is a peaceful place to reflect and observe local worshippers.

Another must-visit is Mount Phousi, a small hill in the center of town that offers panoramic views of Luang Prabang and the surrounding mountains. On top of the hill is a stupa called That Chomsi, and climbing the 300 steps to the top is a rewarding experience, especially at sunrise or sunset.

• **Morning Alms Giving Ceremony**

One of the most sacred traditions in Luang Prabang is the morning alms giving ceremony. Every morning at sunrise, monks walk through the streets collecting food offerings from the local people. This ritual, called Tak Bat, is a quiet and respectful exchange that reflects the strong connection between the monks and the community. As a visitor, you can watch the ceremony, but it's important to be respectful and avoid interrupting the procession. If you wish to participate, you should do so in a thoughtful manner, by dressing appropriately and learning the proper way to give alms.

• **Night Market and Local Crafts**

Luang Prabang also has a vibrant night market, where you can find a wide variety of handicrafts, textiles, and souvenirs made by local artisans. The market comes alive in the evening, with vendors setting up stalls along Sisavangvong Road. It's the perfect place to pick up traditional Lao items such as silk scarves, handmade jewelry, and wooden carvings. Bargaining is common, but always done in a friendly and polite way.

• The map above shows distance (with time covered) from Thailand central location to Luan Prabang

Vientiane

Vientiane, the capital of Laos, is a quiet and charming city that blends old traditions with French colonial influences. Unlike bustling capitals in other countries, Vientiane moves at a slower pace, offering visitors a relaxing atmosphere filled with history, religious landmarks, and peaceful parks. Though smaller in size, it holds many important symbols of Laos' culture and heritage. The following key attractions make Vientiane a must-visit destination:

• **Patuxai Victory Monument**

The Patuxai Victory Monument, sometimes referred to as the "Arc de Triomphe of Laos," is one of Vientiane's most recognizable landmarks. Built between 1957 and 1968, the monument was constructed to honor those who fought for Laos' independence from France. While its design is similar to Paris' Arc de Triomphe, Patuxai has distinctive Lao details, including traditional reliefs and decorations that give it a unique look.

Visitors can climb the stairs inside the monument to reach the top, where they will be treated to panoramic views of the city. The surrounding park area is also a pleasant spot for an afternoon stroll or a relaxing break from sightseeing.

• **Pha That Luang**

Considered the most important national monument in Laos, Pha That Luang is a striking golden stupa that symbolizes the country's Buddhist faith and sovereignty. The stupa is believed to have been originally built in the 3rd century, though it has been rebuilt several times due to invasions and damage. Today, Pha That Luang stands as a symbol of Laotian pride and spirituality.

The stupa is surrounded by various smaller temples and Buddha statues, making it a peaceful place for reflection. Every November, the That Luang Festival is held here, where monks and pilgrims gather to offer prayers and celebrate Laos' Buddhist heritage.

• Buddha Park (Xieng Khuan)

Located about 25 kilometers from Vientiane, Buddha Park is an unusual and fascinating site that attracts visitors with its collection of over 200 religious statues. The park, created by a mystic named Luang Pu Bunleua Sulilat in 1958, features a mix of Buddhist and Hindu imagery, with sculptures of Buddha, deities, demons, and mythological creatures.

One of the park's most interesting structures is a massive, pumpkin-shaped building that represents hell, earth, and heaven. Visitors can climb inside to explore its three levels, each symbolizing a different realm of existence. Buddha Park is both a place of worship and an outdoor museum, offering a unique insight into Lao spiritual beliefs.

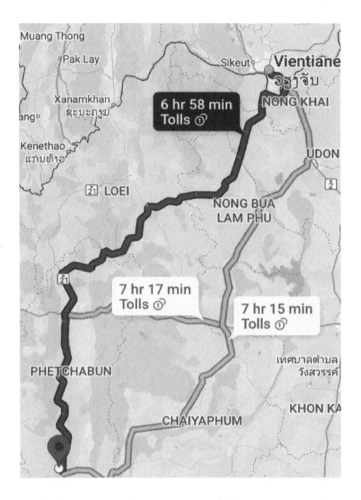

• The map above shows distance (with time covered) from Thailand central location to Vientiane

Vang Vieng

Vang Vieng, located about four hours north of Vientiane, is a popular destination for adventure seekers and nature lovers. The town, once known for its lively backpacker scene, has evolved into a hub for outdoor activities, thanks to its dramatic limestone karsts, winding rivers, and impressive caves. Vang Vieng offers a mix of adrenaline-pumping adventures and peaceful natural beauty.

• **Kayaking and Tubing down of the Nam Song River**

Tubing down of the Nam Song River is one of the most famous and remarkable activities in Vang Vieng. Visitors can float lazily down the river in an inflatable tube, taking in the stunning views of the surrounding mountains and lush greenery. Along the way, there are riverside bars where you can stop for a drink or a snack, making tubing both a relaxing and social experience.

For those looking for a bit more action, kayaking is another great way to explore the river. Paddling through gentle rapids and calm waters, kayakers get up-close views of the beautiful limestone cliffs that line the riverbanks. Whether you prefer the slow pace of tubing or the excitement of kayaking, the Nam Song River is the heart of Vang Vieng's outdoor adventures.

• **Limestone Karsts**

The towering limestone karsts that surround Vang Vieng are a major attraction. These jagged cliffs rise dramatically from the landscape, creating a surreal backdrop for the town. The karsts are not only beautiful to look at, but they also provide opportunities for rock climbing and hiking. Adventurous travelers can take on the challenge of scaling the cliffs or trekking to the top for panoramic views of the valley below.

• **Cave Explorations**

Vang Vieng is home to numerous caves, many of which can be explored by visitors. The caves are filled with stalactites, stalagmites, and underground rivers, offering a unique glimpse into the area's natural wonders.

One of the most famous caves is Tham Chang, which is easily accessible and known for its cool interior and picturesque views of the countryside. Another popular cave is Tham Phu Kham, located near the Blue Lagoon. Inside this cave, there's a reclining Buddha statue, and visitors can swim in the nearby lagoon's crystal-clear waters after their cave exploration.

For those seeking a bit more adventure, there's Tham Nam (Water Cave), where visitors can float through the cave on inner tubes while pulling themselves along with a rope. Exploring the caves of Vang Vieng is a great way to experience both the natural beauty and the mystery of the region.

Si Phan Don (4,000 Islands)

Si Phan Don, or the "4,000 Islands," is a picturesque region in southern Laos where the Mekong River fans out, creating a maze of islands and islets. This tranquil destination offers a peaceful retreat away from the busier cities, perfect for those looking to relax in nature, soak up the local culture, and experience the slow-paced life along the river. With its scenic beauty, friendly locals, and unique wildlife, Si Phan Don is a hidden gem in Laos.

• Mekong River Islands

Si Phan Don's name translates to "4,000 islands," and while not all of them are inhabited, many of the larger islands offer a variety of activities and experiences. The three main islands that attract visitors are Don Khong, Don Det, and Don Khon.

- **Don Khong** is the largest of the islands and offers a more traditional, laid-back atmosphere. It's a great place to bike around, visit small villages, and experience the quiet life of the Mekong.

- **Don Det** is more popular with backpackers due to its budget-friendly guesthouses and vibrant nightlife. Despite its popularity, it still retains a relaxed vibe, with its main attractions being its beautiful sunsets, quiet riverfront, and the chance to rent a bike or kayak to explore the surrounding areas.

- **Don Khon** is known for its natural beauty and historical sites, including the remains of a French colonial railway and stunning waterfalls like Li Phi Falls. It's also the place to spot the famous Irrawaddy dolphins.

• Dolphins and Wildlife

One of the most unique experiences in Si Phan Don is the opportunity to see the rare Irrawaddy dolphins, which are found in the Mekong River between Don Khon and Cambodia.

These freshwater dolphins are an endangered species, and local boat tours offer visitors the chance to spot them in their natural habitat.

Early morning or late afternoon boat trips give the best chance of seeing the dolphins, while also providing a peaceful journey along the river.

Besides dolphins, the islands are home to various species of birds and fish, and visitors can enjoy fishing trips, birdwatching, or simply observing the abundant wildlife along the riverbanks.

• Laid-Back Charm

The charm of Si Phan Don lies in its relaxed pace of life. There are no big hotels or shopping malls here, and the islands' main activities revolve around enjoying the simple pleasures of life: lounging in a hammock, watching the sunset over the Mekong, or taking a leisurely bike ride through rice fields and small villages.

While Si Phan Don may not have the high-energy activities of other tourist destinations, its peaceful environment and natural beauty make it a perfect escape for those looking to unwind.

The friendly locals, welcoming guesthouses, and beautiful scenery ensure that your time here will be both enjoyable and rejuvenating.

Insider travel tips for Laos

Here are some practical travel tips to help you navigate your journey through Laos.

• Cultural Etiquette

Laos has a rich cultural heritage, deeply rooted in Buddhism, and respecting local customs is important when visiting. Here are some important cultural information to keep in mind as you travel:

- Greetings

The traditional Lao greeting is the "nop," where you place your hands together in a prayer-like gesture at chest level and slightly bow your head. It's polite to return this gesture when greeted by locals.

- Respect for Monks and Temples

Monks hold a revered place in Lao society, and visitors should show respect when encountering them.

Women should avoid touching monks or their belongings. When visiting temples, dress modestly, cover your shoulders and knees, and remove your shoes before entering.

- Head and Feet

In Lao culture, the head is considered the most sacred part of the body, while the feet are seen as the lowest. When sitting in a temple, sit cross-legged or with your feet tucked behind you.

- General Etiquette

Lao people value politeness and calmness. Public displays of anger or frustration are frowned upon, and it's always appreciated when travelers show patience and respect for local customs.

• Must-Try Dishes

Lao cuisine is known for its fresh ingredients, bold flavors, and use of herbs and spices. Below are some nice dishes you may have to try out:

- Laap (Larb)

A traditional Lao dish made from minced meat (usually pork, chicken, or fish) mixed with lime juice, fish sauce, herbs, and spices. It's often served with sticky rice and is considered a national dish.

- Tam Mak Hoong (Papaya Salad)

A spicy and tangy salad made from shredded green papaya, tomatoes, lime juice, fish sauce, chili, and garlic. It's a popular street food and can be found all over Laos.

- Khao Niew (Sticky Rice)

Sticky rice is a staple in Lao cuisine and is served with almost every meal. It's often eaten with your hands by rolling small amounts into a ball and dipping it into sauces or pairing it with meats and vegetables.

- Or Lam

A hearty stew made from vegetables, meat (usually buffalo or chicken), and a variety of herbs. It's a comforting dish that reflects the country's use of fresh, local ingredients.

- Khao Piak Sen (Lao Noodle Soup)

A comforting noodle soup made with rice noodles in a flavorful broth, often topped with fresh herbs, lime, and chili.

It's commonly eaten for breakfast but is enjoyed throughout the day.

• Transportation in Laos

Getting around Laos can be a bit challenging due to the country's mountainous terrain and limited infrastructure, but there are several options for travelers:

- Buses and Minivans

The most common mode of long-distance travel in Laos is by bus or minivan. These range from local buses to more comfortable tourist buses.Keep in mind that roads can be bumpy, and travel times may be longer than expected.

- Tuk-Tuks and Songthaews

For short distances within towns, tuk-tuks (motorized rickshaws) and songthaews (shared pickup trucks) are the main forms of transportation.

- Boats

Given the importance of the Mekong River in Laos, boat travel is a popular option, especially for visiting islands like Si Phan Don or exploring river towns like Luang

Prabang. Slow boats and speedboats are available for longer journeys.

- Motorbike Rentals

In many towns and cities, renting a motorbike is a convenient and affordable way to explore the local area. However, be cautious of road conditions, especially in rural areas.

- Flights

For faster travel between major destinations, Laos has a few domestic airlines that operate flights between cities like Vientiane, Luang Prabang, and Pakse.

Chapter Five: Northern Thailand

Chiang Mai

Chiang Mai is located in Northern Thailand. Known as the "Rose of the North," it has

---

become a favorite destination for travelers seeking a balance between tradition and modernity. From its ancient temples and bustling night markets to the nearby hill tribe villages, Chiang Mai offers a unique glimpse into Thailand's past and present.

• Temples

The city of Chiang Mai is home to many spiritual temples. The city's temples are a reflection of its deep-rooted Buddhist traditions and spiritual importance.

- Wat Phra That Doi Suthep

Perched on a mountain overlooking the city, this temple is one of Chiang Mai's most famous landmarks. It offers stunning views of the city below and is a pilgrimage site for many Buddhists.

Visitors can climb the 300 steps or take a tram to reach the temple, where they can admire the golden stupa and intricate carvings.

- Wat Chedi Luang

Located in the heart of Chiang Mai's Old City, Wat Chedi Luang is an ancient temple dating back to the 14th century. Its large chedi (stupa) once stood at 82 meters tall before being partially destroyed by an earthquake. The temple grounds are peaceful, and visitors can also see the city pillar shrine.

- Wat Phra Singh

Another important temple in the Old City, Wat Phra Singh is known for its beautiful Lanna-style architecture and the revered Phra Singh Buddha image. The temple complex includes several buildings, and it's an excellent example of Northern Thai craftsmanship.

• Night Markets

Chiang Mai is famous for its vibrant night markets, where visitors can shop for handmade crafts, clothing, and souvenirs while sampling delicious street food.

The night markets are a great place to experience the local culture and find unique items.

- Sunday Walking Street

This popular market stretches along Ratchadamnoen Road in the Old City every Sunday evening.

Vendors set up stalls selling everything from traditional handicrafts and jewelry to art and home decor.

The market also features street performances and food stalls offering local delicacies like khao soi (curry noodle soup) and mango sticky rice.

- Night Bazaar

Located on Chang Klan Road, the Night Bazaar is a bustling marketplace open every night.

It's a great spot to shop for souvenirs, clothes, and electronics.

The bazaar also has a food court with a wide variety of Thai and international dishes, making it a favorite among both tourists and locals.

• Hill Tribe Villages

One of the most unique experiences in Chiang Mai is visiting the hill tribe villages that are located in the mountains surrounding the city.

These communities belong to various ethnic groups, including the Hmong, Karen, Akha, and Lahu tribes, each with its own language, customs, and traditions.

191

- Karen Long Neck Village

The Karen people are famous for their women who wear brass rings around their necks, which create the appearance of an elongated neck. Visitors can learn about their lifestyle, traditional crafts, and the significance of this practice. It's important to approach these visits with respect and understanding, as some villages may rely on tourism for income.

- Hmong Hill Tribe

The Hmong people live in villages scattered across the hills around Chiang Mai. They are known for their colorful embroidered clothing and intricate handicrafts. Visitors can take guided tours to experience the daily life of the Hmong people, learn about their agricultural practices, and purchase handmade textiles.

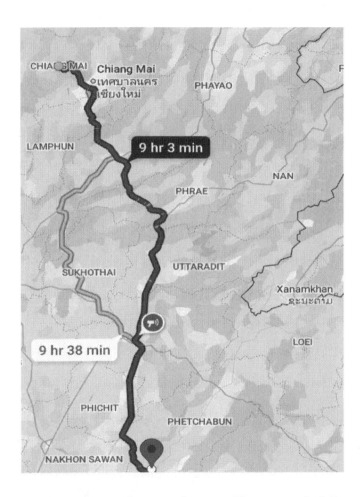

• The map above shows distance (with time covered) from Thailand central location to Chiang Mai

Chiang Rai

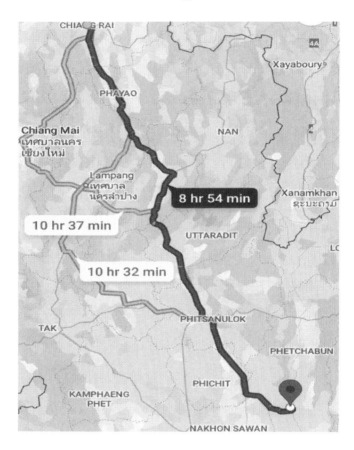

• **The map above shows distance (with time covered) from Thailand central location to Chiang Rai**

This city is located further north from Chiang Mai. It's known for its remarkable temples and its proximity to the Golden Triangle, where Thailand, Laos, and Myanmar meet. Chiang Rai offers a quieter atmosphere compared to Chiang Mai, but it is packed with fascinating sites and cultural experiences.

• **The White Temple (Wat Rong Khun)**

Wat Rong Khun, commonly known as the White Temple, is one of the most famous landmarks in Thailand. Designed by artist Chalermchai Kositpipat, this stunning temple is unlike any other in the country. Its gleaming white exterior is adorned with intricate carvings and mirror mosaics, giving it a surreal, otherworldly appearance.

The temple represents the path to enlightenment, and visitors must cross a bridge over a sea of outstretched hands symbolizing desire before entering the temple. Inside, the artwork combines traditional Buddhist elements with modern pop culture references, making it a unique blend of old and new.

• The Blue Temple (Wat Rong Suea Ten)

Another visually striking temple in Chiang Rai is Wat Rong Suea Ten, known as the Blue Temple due to its deep blue and gold color scheme. The temple's design is equally breathtaking, with intricate details and bold colors that set it apart from other temples in the region.

The interior of the temple is dominated by a massive white Buddha statue, while the walls are adorned with beautiful murals.

The temple's serene atmosphere and unique color palette make it a favorite among visitors seeking a peaceful and visually stunning experience.

• The Golden Triangle

The Golden Triangle is the area where Thailand, Laos, and Myanmar converge along the Mekong River. Historically, the region was known for its role in the opium trade, but today it is a popular tourist destination offering insights into the region's history and culture.

- Golden Triangle Park

Visitors can take a boat ride along the Mekong River to see the point where the three countries meet. There's also a viewpoint where you can overlook the confluence of the rivers and the surrounding landscapes.

The area is also home to several museums, including the Hall of Opium, which provides a detailed history of the opium trade and its impact on the region.

- Local Villages and Markets

The Golden Triangle area is home to various ethnic minority groups, and visitors can explore the local villages and markets to experience traditional crafts, textiles, and daily life.

It's a great opportunity to learn about the cultures of the people living in this unique border region.

Sukhothai

Sukhothai, which means "Dawn of Happiness," is one of Thailand's most significant historical sites.

As the first capital of the Kingdom of Siam, it holds a special place in Thai history and culture.

Founded in the 13th century, Sukhothai is often regarded as the birthplace of Thai art, architecture, and language.

Today, the ancient city is a UNESCO World Heritage site, known for its well-preserved ruins and serene atmosphere.

• **Sukhothai Historical Park**

The Sukhothai Historical Park is the main attraction, where the ruins of the old city provide a glimpse into the grandeur of the Sukhothai Kingdom.

Spread over 70 square kilometers, the park is home to temples, palaces, and Buddha statues that reflect the architectural style of the era.

- Wat Mahathat

The largest and most important temple in Sukhothai, Wat Mahathat was once the spiritual center of the city.

The temple complex features a large seated Buddha statue and numerous stupas.

The intricate stone carvings and lotus-shaped stupas showcase the artistry of the Sukhothai period.

- Wat Si Chum

Known for its massive seated Buddha, this temple is one of the most iconic sites in Sukhothai.

The Buddha, measuring 15 meters tall, sits within a narrow mondop (square building), creating a peaceful and awe-inspiring sight.

- Wat Saphan Hin

Located on a hill just outside the main city area, Wat Saphan Hin offers panoramic views of the surrounding countryside.

Visitors can climb a stone path to reach the temple, where a standing Buddha statue watches over the landscape.

• Exploring the Ancient City

Visitors can explore the Sukhothai Historical Park by foot, bicycle, or even by electric cart. Biking through the park is a popular way to take in the beauty of the ruins while enjoying the peaceful surroundings. The park's tranquil atmosphere, with its lotus-filled ponds, shaded trees, and quiet pathways, makes it a perfect place to slow down and reflect on Thailand's rich history.

In addition to the historical park, Sukhothai is also known for its traditional crafts, including pottery and textiles. Travelers can visit local artisans to see how these traditional crafts are still practiced today.

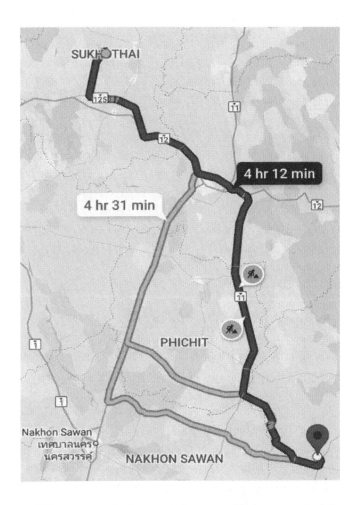

• **The map above shows distance (with time covered) from Thailand central location to Sukhothai**

Mae Hong Son

This is located in the far northwest of Thailand near the border with Myanmar. It's a province famous for its stunning mountain landscapes, remote villages, and rich cultural diversity. The region's rugged terrain and cooler climate make it a favorite destination for nature lovers and adventurers seeking to experience a more peaceful and authentic side of Thailand.

• Mountain Landscapes and Nature

The natural beauty of Mae Hong Son is one of its greatest draws. The province is home to lush forests, rolling hills, and scenic viewpoints that provide a sense of serenity and isolation.

- Pai Canyon

Pai Canyon, located near the town of Pai, offers breathtaking views of the surrounding countryside. The narrow ridges and deep valleys create a dramatic landscape that's perfect for hiking and photography. The canyon is particularly beautiful at sunrise and sunset when the golden light casts a warm glow over the landscape.

- Tham Lod Cave

This massive limestone cave is one of Mae Hong Son's natural wonders. Visitors can explore the cave by walking and by bamboo raft, guided by locals with lanterns. Inside the cave, there are ancient stalactites, stalagmites, and even prehistoric cave paintings.

- Pang Ung Lake

Known as the "Switzerland of Thailand," Pang Ung is a peaceful lake surrounded by pine trees and mist-covered hills. Visitors can enjoy boating on the lake or simply relax and take in the serene atmosphere.

• Cultural Experiences

Mae Hong Son is home to several ethnic minority groups, including the Shan, Karen, and Hmong, each with their own traditions, language, and customs. These hill tribe communities offer visitors a unique cultural experience, allowing them to learn about different ways of life that have been preserved for centuries.

- Karen Long Neck Villages

The Karen people, known for their women who wear brass rings around their necks, have become a symbol of the region. Visitors can learn about their traditional crafts, such as weaving and wood carving, and gain an understanding of their unique cultural practices.

- Shan Influence

Mae Hong Son has strong cultural ties to Myanmar, particularly among the Shan people. The city of Mae Hong Son itself has a distinct Burmese influence, seen in the architecture of temples like Wat Chong

Kham and Wat Chong Klang, which are situated near the scenic Chong Kham Lake.

• **Pai Town**

Pai is a small town in Mae Hong Son Province that has gained popularity among backpackers and nature lovers. Known for its laid-back vibe, Pai offers a mix of natural beauty and modern comforts. The town is surrounded by hot springs, waterfalls, and picturesque valleys, making it a great base for outdoor activities like trekking, cycling, and rafting.

Pai is also famous for its night market, where visitors can enjoy delicious street food, browse local crafts, and soak in the town's bohemian atmosphere. The town's lively yet relaxed ambiance makes it a perfect place to unwind after a day of exploring the surrounding countryside.

Insider travel tips for Northern Thailand

To help you make the most of your visit, here are some insider tips on local traditions, top hiking spots, and the delicious food of Northern Thailand.

• Local Traditions and Customs

Northern Thailand has its own distinct cultural identity, influenced by its historical connection to the ancient Lanna Kingdom and its proximity to neighboring Myanmar and Laos. Understanding the region's traditions and customs will help you appreciate the local way of life and ensure respectful interactions with the people.

- Respect for Temples

Temples (or "wats") play an important role in Thai culture. When you visit temples, your shoes should be removed before entering, and you should avoid pointing your feet towards Buddha statues, as it is considered disrespectful.

- Loy Krathong and Yi Peng Festivals

If you visit Northern Thailand in November, don't miss the Loy Krathong and Yi Peng festivals. Loy Krathong involves floating small decorated baskets (krathongs) on rivers and lakes, while Yi Peng is famous for releasing thousands of paper lanterns into the sky. These festivals are magical to witness and provide a deep connection to local spiritual beliefs.

- Hill Tribe Villages

The northern region is home to various hill tribe communities, including the Karen, Hmong, and Lisu people. Many of these groups maintain their traditional clothing, crafts, and farming practices. While visiting their villages, it's important to be respectful of their customs and avoid taking pictures of people without their permission. Purchasing handmade textiles or crafts directly from the villages can support their communities.

• Best Hiking Spots in Northern Thailand

For nature lovers, Northern Thailand is a paradise of mountains, forests, and waterfalls. Whether you're looking for challenging treks or scenic walks, the region offers many stunning hiking trails. Below are some of the best hiking spots worth recommending for you, as a traveler:

- Doi Inthanon National Park

This is known as the highest mountain in the country. The national park surrounding the mountain is a popular destination for trekking. Trails wind through dense forests, passing waterfalls, hill tribe villages, and viewpoints with panoramic vistas.

- Doi Suthep-Pui National Park

Just outside of Chiang Mai, Doi Suthep-Pui National Park offers several hiking options. The trek up to Wat Phra That Doi Suthep, a beautiful temple with views over the city, is one of the most popular.

For those looking for a more challenging hike, the trails leading up to Doi Pui and Huay Tung Tao Lake provide stunning scenery and a peaceful retreat from the city.

- Mae Hong Son Loop

This scenic route through the mountains offers many opportunities for hiking and exploring nature.

Pai Canyon is a must-visit for its breathtaking views and narrow ridges, while Tham Lod Cave provides a unique combination of hiking and caving, with the option to explore the cave by bamboo raft.

- Chiang Dao

Chiang Dao is known for its limestone mountains and caves. Doi Chiang Dao, Thailand's third-highest peak, is a challenging hike that rewards climbers with stunning views of the surrounding landscape. For those interested in a less strenuous adventure, the Chiang Dao Cave system offers an easier exploration with ancient Buddha statues and impressive rock formations.

• Cuisine in Northern Thailand

Northern Thai cuisine is distinct from other regional Thai cuisines, featuring bold flavors, sticky rice, and plenty of herbs. The food reflects the region's cooler climate and mountainous terrain, with influences from neighboring countries like Myanmar and Laos. Below are some nice dishes you will love in no small way:

- Khao Soi

One of the most famous dishes in Northern Thailand, Khao Soi is a curry noodle soup made with coconut milk, crispy fried noodles, and tender meat (usually chicken or beef). It's rich and flavorful, with a balance of spicy, tangy, and creamy tastes.

- Sai Ua (Northern Thai Sausage)

Sai Ua is a grilled pork sausage seasoned with herbs like lemongrass, kaffir lime leaves, and galangal. It's often served with sticky rice and makes for a delicious snack or side dish.

- Laab

Laab is a type of meat salad made with minced pork, chicken, or beef, mixed with fresh herbs, lime juice, and roasted rice powder. In Northern Thailand, you'll often find Laab Muang, which has a spicier and more herbal flavor compared to the version found in other parts of Thailand.

- Nam Prik Noom

This spicy green chili dip is a staple in Northern Thai cuisine. It's made from roasted green chilies, garlic, and shallots, and is typically eaten with sticky rice and fresh or steamed vegetables.

- Sticky Rice

Unlike in central and southern Thailand, where jasmine rice is the staple, sticky rice (or khao niaow) is the preferred accompaniment to meals in the north. It's often served in small bamboo baskets and is eaten by hand.

- Kaeng Hang Lei

This rich and savory pork curry is a specialty of the north, known for its slow-cooked tenderness and flavorful sauce made from tamarind, garlic, and ginger.

• **Final Tips for Traveling in Northern Thailand**

- Transportation

In Northern Thailand, the best way to get around is by motorbike, car rental, or public transportation. Chiang Mai and Chiang Rai have airports with domestic and international flights, but to explore the smaller towns and villages, buses or shared vans (songthaews) are the primary means of transportation.

- Language

While Thai is the official language, many locals, especially in tourist areas like Chiang Mai, speak some English. Learning a few basic Thai phrases like "sawasdee" (hello) and "khop khun" (thank you) will be appreciated by locals.

- Cultural Etiquette

In addition to respecting temples, it's important to dress modestly, particularly when visiting rural areas and hill tribe villages. Avoid raising your voice or showing frustration, as maintaining "face" is important in Thai culture.

- Safety

Northern Thailand is generally very safe for tourists, but it's always a good idea to be cautious with personal belongings, particularly in crowded areas like markets. When hiking, make sure to follow marked trails and bring plenty of water, especially in the dry season when it can get hot.

Chapter Six: 7-Day Itinerary

Day 1: Hanoi, Vietnam

Welcome to Hanoi, the bustling capital of Vietnam! After you arrive and settle into your accommodation, take a moment to soak in the energy of this vibrant city. Hanoi, known for its blend of ancient history and modern life, is the perfect starting point for your Southeast Asia adventure.

• **Exploring the Old Quarter**

Your first stop should be Hanoi's famous Old Quarter, the heart of the city's cultural and commercial life. The Old Quarter is a maze of narrow streets, each one historically named after the specific trade or goods that were sold there, such as Hang Bac (Silver Street) or Hang Gai (Silk Street). Today, it's a lively area full of shops, markets, cafes, and street vendors.

Wander through the streets at your own pace, and you'll see colonial architecture mixed with traditional Vietnamese tube houses. Be sure to explore the bustling street markets where you can buy anything from souvenirs to local snacks. The area is great for people-watching, as you'll witness the everyday life of Hanoi's residents, from vendors selling fruit on bicycles to locals sitting on tiny plastic stools enjoying a bowl of pho.

• **Hoan Kiem Lake**

After exploring the Old Quarter, head over to Hoan Kiem Lake, just a short walk away. This peaceful lake is an iconic part of Hanoi's landscape and a favorite spot for locals to gather. The lake is not only a place of relaxation but also holds historical and cultural significance.

In the middle of the lake, you'll see the small Turtle Tower on a tiny island. According to legend, a golden turtle god helped King Le Loi defeat the Chinese Ming dynasty by lending him a magical sword, which he returned to the lake after the victory.

While strolling around the lake, don't forget to visit the Ngoc Son Temple, a small but beautiful temple located on another island in the lake, connected by the bright red Huc Bridge. The temple honors various figures, including General Tran Hung Dao, a national hero known for defeating Mongol invaders in the 13th century.

• **Evening: Traditional Water Puppet Show**

As evening falls, make your way to a traditional water puppet show. Water puppetry is a unique art form that originated in northern Vietnam centuries ago. The puppets are controlled by puppeteers standing waist-deep in water, and the show tells stories of rural life, legends, and folklore, often accompanied by live music. The Thang Long Water Puppet Theatre is one of the best places you can experience that. It's located near Hoan Kiem Lake.

The show typically lasts about an hour and provides a fascinating glimpse into Vietnamese culture and history. Even if you don't understand the Vietnamese language, the visual storytelling and music make it enjoyable for all ages.

• **Street Food Tasting**

After the show, it's time to dive into Hanoi's famous street food scene. Hanoi is renowned for its delicious and affordable street food, and the Old Quarter is the best place to try it. You can either join a guided street food tour or explore on your own. Either way, be sure to try some of these classic Vietnamese dishes:

- Pho

Vietnam's most famous dish, a flavorful noodle soup with beef or chicken, typically served with fresh herbs, lime, and chili.

- Banh Mi

A Vietnamese-style sandwich made with a crispy baguette filled with meats, pickled vegetables, and fresh herbs.

- Bun Cha

This is grilled pork usually served with rice noodles, herbs, and a dipping sauce. It's a Hanoi specialty!

- Nem Ran

Crispy fried spring rolls filled with vegetables, pork, or seafood.

For dessert, try Che, a sweet Vietnamese pudding made with various ingredients like beans, coconut milk, and fruit, or cool off with some freshly made sugarcane juice or egg coffee, a unique Hanoi creation.

Day 2: Ha Long Bay, Vietnam

• **Morning**

After breakfast in Hanoi, prepare for an exciting day trip to Ha Long Bay, one of Vietnam's most famous natural wonders and a UNESCO World Heritage Site.

Most tours start early, so you'll board a bus or shuttle that takes you through the scenic countryside, approximately a 3.5 to 4-hour drive from Hanoi.

As you travel, enjoy the views of lush green rice fields, charming villages, and the stunning landscapes of northern Vietnam.

Your guide will share interesting facts about the area, making the journey enjoyable and informative.

• Arrival at Ha Long Bay

Upon reaching Ha Long Bay, you'll board a traditional wooden junk boat that will be your home for the day. The crew will welcome you aboard, and you'll have a chance to get comfortable while admiring the breathtaking scenery.

• Day Cruise Through Ha Long Bay

As your boat sets sail, get ready to explore the stunning beauty of Ha Long Bay. The cruise will take you through the bay's myriad islands, each with its unique shapes and stories. Keep your camera ready as you glide past the famous islands like Thien Cung (Heavenly Palace Cave) and Dau Go (Wooden Stakes Island).

• Visiting Caves

Your first stop will likely be one of the magnificent caves in Ha Long Bay.

The most popular choices are Sung Sot (Surprise Cave) or Thien Cung (Heavenly Palace Cave). Sung Sot Cave is known for its impressive size and the stunning formations inside. As you walk through, you'll see various stalactites and stalagmites that resemble animals and mythical creatures. The cave has two main chambers, and as you explore, your guide will share stories and legends about the cave's history.

In contrast, Thien Cung Cave features vibrant stalactites and colorful lighting that create a magical atmosphere. Take your time exploring the unique formations and learning about their origins.

• **Kayaking Adventure**

After visiting the caves, it's time for some adventure! You'll have the chance to go kayaking in the calm waters of the bay. This is an amazing way to get closer to the towering limestone cliffs and explore hidden lagoons. Kayaking allows you to paddle around small islands and enjoy the tranquility of the bay. Keep an eye out for local wildlife, including colorful birds and playful monkeys, as you navigate through the stunning scenery.

If you prefer, some tours may offer a swim stop at a quiet beach, where you can enjoy the refreshing waters of the Gulf of Tonkin.

• **Lunch on the Boat**

While you're cruising through the bay, enjoy a delicious lunch on board. Most cruises serve a variety of traditional Vietnamese dishes, including spring rolls, fried fish, and stir-fried vegetables, all made with fresh local ingredients.

Savor your meal while taking in the stunning views of limestone islands dotted around you.

- **Afternoon: More Sightseeing and Return to Hanoi**

After lunch, continue your cruise around Ha Long Bay. Your captain will navigate through some of the most scenic areas, giving you plenty of opportunities to take photos. You may also have time to visit a small fishing village or a pearl farm to learn about local fishing practices and the production of beautiful pearl jewelry.

As the afternoon sun begins to set, the bay's beauty transforms into something truly magical. The soft golden light casts a warm glow on the limestone islands, making for perfect photo opportunities.

- **Evening: Return to Hanoi or Overnight Cruise**

After a fulfilling day of exploration, your cruise will start making its way back to the harbor. Once you arrive, you'll have a choice to make: you can either return to Hanoi by bus or opt for an overnight cruise on Ha Long Bay.

If you choose to return to Hanoi, you'll enjoy a relaxing ride back to the city, reflecting on the day's adventures and the stunning sights you've seen. Once back in Hanoi, you can have dinner at a local restaurant or explore the city a bit more.

If you decide to stay on a cruise, you can enjoy a serene evening surrounded by the peaceful waters of Ha Long Bay. Most overnight cruises provide dinner and evening activities, such as cooking classes or squid fishing, allowing you to experience more of the bay's beauty under the stars.

Day 3: Phnom Penh, Cambodia

• **Morning**

Start your day with breakfast in Hanoi, enjoying a delicious bowl of pho or fresh spring rolls before heading to the airport for your short flight to Phnom Penh, the capital city of Cambodia. The flight typically takes about an hour and offers stunning views of the landscape below as you transition from Vietnam to Cambodia.

Upon arrival at Phnom Penh International Airport, you will go through customs and collect your luggage. Once you exit the airport, you can take a taxi or arrange for a hotel transfer to get to your accommodation in the city.

• **Late Morning: Visit the Royal Palace**

After checking in at your hotel, get ready to explore the heart of Cambodia's capital. Your first stop is the Royal Palace, a magnificent complex that serves as the residence of the King of Cambodia. The palace grounds are filled with beautiful

231

gardens, intricate buildings, and vibrant colors.

As you wander through the palace grounds, you'll see the Silver Pagoda, named for its floor covered in over 5,000 silver tiles. Inside, you can admire a stunning collection of Buddha statues made from various materials, including gold and crystal.

Make sure to take your time to appreciate the architectural details and the peaceful atmosphere of the palace. If you're lucky, you might catch a glimpse of the royal family or witness a ceremonial event taking place.

• Lunch: Local Cambodian Cuisine

After your visit to the Royal Palace, enjoy lunch at a nearby restaurant or a local market. This is the perfect time to try some traditional Khmer dishes. Popular choices include amok (a coconut milk curry), loc lac (stir-fried beef served with rice), and nom banh chok (Cambodian rice noodle salad). Be sure to sip on a refreshing coconut water or fresh fruit juice to keep cool.

• Afternoon: Tuol Sleng Museum

Following lunch, head to the Tuol Sleng Genocide Museum, a somber but important site that provides insight into Cambodia's tragic history. This former high school was converted into a prison and interrogation center during the Khmer Rouge regime from 1975 to 1979.

As you enter the museum, you will see displays of photographs and artifacts that tell the stories of the people who suffered here.

Guided tours are available and are highly recommended, as the guides can share powerful narratives about the events that took place. It's a moving experience that helps you understand Cambodia's past and the resilience of its people.

• **Evening**

As the day winds down, get ready for a relaxing sunset cruise on the Mekong River. This is a perfect way to unwind and soak in the beauty of the city as the sun sets over the water.

Many companies offer boat tours that provide stunning views of the riverside, including the Royal Palace and the lively riverside promenade.

On the cruise, you can sit back and enjoy the gentle breeze while taking photographs of the changing colors of the sky. Some tours may offer snacks or drinks, allowing you to savor the moment even more.

As night falls, the city lights begin to twinkle, and you can enjoy the sights of

Phnom Penh as it comes alive in the evening. It's a peaceful and reflective way to end a day filled with culture and history.

• **Dinner: Traditional Cambodian Dining**

After your cruise, head back to the riverside area for dinner. There are many restaurants that offer both local and international cuisine. Consider trying a Khmer barbecue or a buffet that features various Cambodian dishes.

As you enjoy your meal, take in the lively atmosphere of the city, with street vendors selling snacks and locals enjoying the evening.

Day 4: Siem Reap, Cambodia

• **Early Morning: Tour of Angkor Wat and Surrounding Temples.**

Wake up early and prepare for an unforgettable adventure to Siem Reap, home of the magnificent Angkor Wat temple complex. After a quick breakfast, you'll want to head out to catch the sunrise at Angkor Wat, one of the most iconic sights in Cambodia.

As you arrive at the temple, you'll witness the breathtaking view of the sun rising behind the towering spires of Angkor Wat. This moment is magical, as the temple reflects beautifully on the surrounding water. Make sure to bring your camera to capture this stunning scene!

After sunrise, you'll enter Angkor Wat, a UNESCO World Heritage site and the largest religious monument in the world. Built in the 12th century, Angkor Wat was originally dedicated to the Hindu god Vishnu before becoming a Buddhist temple.

As you walk through its corridors, admire the intricate carvings that depict stories from Hindu mythology, as well as the impressive architecture that showcases the brilliance of the Khmer Empire.

• Late Morning

Next, make your way to Angkor Thom, the last capital of the Khmer Empire. Enter through the impressive South Gate, flanked by giant statues that represent the battle between gods and demons. As you drive or walk through the ancient gates, you'll feel a sense of stepping back in time.

Once inside Angkor Thom, your first stop will be the Bayon Temple, known for its many serene and massive stone faces. The temple is a stunning display of the artistic skills of the Khmer builders. As you explore, you'll notice the intricate bas-reliefs depicting scenes of daily life and historical events, providing a glimpse into the past.

Take your time to walk around and discover the smaller temples within Angkor Thom, like the Baphuon and the Phimeanakas, before heading back to Siem Reap for some relaxation.

• **Lunch: Local Cambodian Cuisine**

After your morning of exploration, it's time to refuel with a delicious lunch. You can find many local restaurants in Siem Reap that serve traditional Khmer dishes. Try amok (a fragrant coconut curry), or fish curry, paired with rice. If you're feeling adventurous, opt for some grilled skewers from a street vendor, which are a popular snack in the area.

• **Afternoon: Relaxation or Visit Local Markets**

Once you've filled up on food, you can choose how to spend your afternoon. If you want to relax, head back to your hotel for some downtime by the pool or a soothing spa treatment. Many hotels in Siem Reap offer excellent spa services, where you can enjoy a traditional Khmer massage and unwind after a busy morning.

If you prefer to explore, visit one of the local markets. The Siem Reap Night Market is a great place to shop for unique souvenirs, handicrafts, and clothing. You'll find items made by local artisans, such as silk scarves, wood carvings, and traditional jewelry. Bargaining is common here, so don't hesitate to negotiate a fair price!

- **Evening: Dinner and Local Entertainment**

As evening approaches, it's time to experience Siem Reap's vibrant nightlife. Choose a local restaurant for dinner, where you can continue to enjoy delicious Cambodian cuisine. Some restaurants even offer cultural performances during dinner, showcasing traditional music and dance.

After dinner, consider visiting a local show that features traditional Apsara dance, a classical dance form that tells stories through graceful movements and colorful costumes.

Day 5: Luang Prabang, Laos

• Morning

Start your day early as you prepare for a flight from Siem Reap to Luang Prabang, a charming town in Laos known for its beautiful landscapes and rich culture. After you're done with your morning breakfast, head to the airport where you would be taking flight. The journey is short, and soon you'll find yourself in this UNESCO World Heritage site, famous for its well-preserved temples and French colonial architecture.

• Arrival in Luang Prabang

Upon arrival, you'll be greeted by the warm hospitality of the Laotian people. Take a moment to soak in the serene atmosphere of the town, which sits at the confluence of the Mekong and Nam Khan rivers. The surroundings are lush and mountainous, creating a picturesque setting that feels like stepping into a postcard.

• **Late Morning: Visit the Royal Palace Museum**

Your first stop in Luang Prabang is the Royal Palace Museum (Haw Kham), the former residence of the Laotian royal family. The museum showcases a fascinating collection of artifacts that reflect the country's royal history, culture, and traditions. As you walk through the museum, you'll see royal regalia, traditional costumes, and gifts from foreign dignitaries. Don't miss the beautiful throne room, which is adorned with intricate murals and gold leaf.

• Afternoon

Next, visit Wat Xieng Thong, one of the most important temples in Luang Prabang. This stunning temple is known for its beautiful architecture and vibrant mosaics. As you enter the temple grounds, you'll notice the intricate designs that tell stories of Buddhist teachings.

Spend some time wandering around the temple complex, taking in the peaceful atmosphere and the beautiful gardens. You can also explore the smaller shrines nearby, each with its own unique charm and history. The atmosphere here is tranquil, making it a perfect spot to reflect and enjoy the beauty of the surroundings.

• Lunch: Enjoy Local Laotian Cuisine

After your visit to Wat Xieng Thong, it's time for lunch. Head to a local restaurant and try some traditional Laotian dishes. A popular choice is larb, a spicy minced meat salad mixed with herbs and spices. You might also want to sample khao soi, a flavorful noodle soup that is a local favorite. Don't forget to sip on some Lao beer or fresh fruit shakes to cool off.

• **Afternoon**

After lunch, take some time to stroll through the charming streets of Luang Prabang. The town is known for its French colonial architecture, so keep your camera handy to capture the beautifully restored buildings, cafes, and shops. You can stop by local artisan shops to see crafts like silk weaving and pottery, where you might find a unique souvenir to take home.

• **Evening: Sunset at Mount Phousi**

As the day winds down, make your way to Mount Phousi for a breathtaking sunset view. Climbing the 328 steps to the top is well worth the effort, as you'll be rewarded with panoramic views of Luang Prabang and the surrounding rivers and mountains. The sunset paints the sky in vibrant hues of orange and pink, creating a magical scene that you won't forget.

At the summit, take a moment to appreciate the beauty of this peaceful town and reflect on your journey. It's a perfect spot to relax and soak in the moment before heading back down.

- **Dinner: Traditional Meal and Night Market**

After descending from Mount Phousi, treat yourself to dinner at a local restaurant. You can try more Laotian specialties, such as sticky rice served with grilled meats or tam mak hoong, a spicy green papaya salad.

After dinner, explore the Luang Prabang Night Market, where local artisans sell their handmade crafts, textiles, and delicious street food. The market is lively and colorful, with various stalls to browse through. It's a great place to pick up unique souvenirs and try some local snacks.

Day 6: Chiang Mai, Thailand

• Morning: Flight to Chiang Mai

On Day 6, you will wake up early to catch a flight from Luang Prabang to Chiang Mai, Thailand's northern capital. This vibrant city is known for its rich history, stunning temples, and beautiful mountains surrounding it. The flight is typically short and comfortable, allowing you to enjoy the views of the changing landscapes as you approach Chiang Mai.

• Arrival in Chiang Mai

Once you arrive in Chiang Mai, take a moment to breathe in the fresh mountain air and feel the city's welcoming atmosphere. You will likely notice the blend of traditional Thai culture and modern conveniences as you make your way to your hotel. After checking in, get ready to explore this fascinating city.

• **Late Morning: Exploring the Old City Temples**

Start your exploration in the Old City, a historic area filled with beautiful temples and ancient walls. One of the first stops is Wat Phra Singh, one of the most revered temples in Chiang Mai. The temple complex features stunning Lanna architecture, intricate carvings, and beautiful murals. Be sure to take your time to appreciate the serene atmosphere and the beautiful Buddha statues.

Next, head to Wat Chedi Luang, a temple known for its impressive ancient chedi, which dates back to the 14th century. Here, you can see the remains of the original structure, which was once the tallest building in the city. Spend some time wandering around the temple grounds and marveling at the unique blend of history and spirituality.

• **Lunch: Enjoy Local Cuisine**

After visiting the temples, it's time to grab lunch at a nearby local eatery. Chiang Mai is famous for its delicious food, so don't miss the chance to try khao soi, a coconut curry noodle soup that is a must-try dish in the region. Pair it with some som tam (spicy papaya salad) or larb (spicy minced meat salad) for a complete meal. Enjoy your meal as you take in the sights and sounds of the Old City.

• **Afternoon: Visit Doi Suthep**

After lunch, set off to Doi Suthep, a mountain located just outside the city. This sacred site is home to the stunning Wat Phra That Doi Suthep, a temple that offers breathtaking views of Chiang Mai from its hillside location. The temple is known for its golden stupa and intricate carvings, making it a significant cultural and spiritual site for the local people.

To reach the temple, you can either take a songthaew (a shared taxi) or opt for a short hike if you're feeling adventurous. Once you arrive, take the time to explore the temple grounds and soak in the peaceful atmosphere. Don't forget to snap some pictures of the stunning views of the city below.

• **Evening: Traditional Lanna Khantoke Dinner**

As the sun begins to set, it's time to enjoy a traditional Lanna Khantoke dinner. This cultural experience allows you to taste a variety of Northern Thai dishes while enjoying traditional music and dance performances. The dinner is served in a unique way, with food placed on a low table called a khantoke.

During the meal, you can try different dishes such as naem (Northern Thai sausage), mushroom curry, and sticky rice. As you eat, watch traditional dancers perform folk dances that celebrate the rich cultural heritage of the Lanna people.

This dinner is not just a meal; it's a cultural celebration that brings together food, music, and dance, offering you a deeper understanding of the traditions of Northern Thailand.

Day 7: Chiang Rai & Golden Triangle, Thailand

• **Morning: Day Trip to Chiang Rai**

On the final day of your journey, you will embark on an exciting day trip to Chiang Rai, a city known for its unique temples and beautiful landscapes. After enjoying breakfast at your hotel in Chiang Mai, meet your guide or hop on a pre-arranged tour bus to start the day. The drive to Chiang Rai takes about three hours, allowing you to see the lush green countryside of Northern Thailand as you travel.

• **First Stop**

Your first destination will be the famous Wat Rong Khun, commonly known as the White Temple. This stunning temple is unlike any other in Thailand, designed by artist Chalermchai Kositpipat. The all-white exterior symbolizes purity and the use of mirrored glass pieces adds a magical touch, reflecting light in all directions. As you approach the temple, you'll see intricate sculptures and paintings that combine traditional Thai elements with contemporary themes, including images from popular culture.

Take your time to explore the temple grounds, marvel at the striking details, and snap plenty of photos. Inside, you'll find murals that tell stories of good and evil, making it a thought-provoking experience. The combination of artistry and spirituality makes the White Temple a must-visit site.

• Next Stop

After visiting the White Temple, head to Wat Rong Suea Ten, also known as the Blue Temple.

This temple features a stunning blue color scheme that sets it apart from the traditional gold and red of many Thai temples. The vibrant blue walls and intricate designs create a striking contrast against the lush green landscape.

As you enter the temple, take a moment to admire the enormous white Buddha statue that sits inside, surrounded by beautiful murals. The Blue Temple is a place of peace and reflection, and you can feel the calm atmosphere as you wander around the grounds.

• Lunch: Enjoy Local Cuisine

After your visit to the Blue Temple, it's time for lunch. Enjoy a meal at a local restaurant where you can try khao soi or other Northern Thai dishes. If you're adventurous, you might also want to sample some kanom jeen (fermented rice noodles) served with a variety of curries and fresh vegetables. The warm hospitality and delicious flavors will be a delightful way to recharge for the rest of the day.

• Afternoon: Golden Triangle Region

Following lunch, make your way to the Golden Triangle, an area where the borders of Thailand, Laos, and Myanmar meet. This historically significant region was once known for opium trade, but today it is a popular tourist destination due to its beautiful scenery and cultural significance.

At the Golden Triangle viewpoint, you'll get a chance to see the convergence of the Mekong and Ruak rivers.

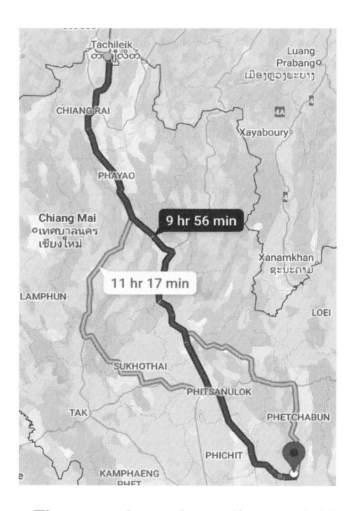

- The map above shows distance (with time covered) from Thailand central location to Golden triangle

Here, you can take in the views and snap some photos of the scenic landscape that stretches out before you. There is also a small museum dedicated to the history of the area and the opium trade if you're interested in learning more.

If time permits, consider visiting Mae Fah Luang Art and Cultural Park, where you can learn about the local culture and admire beautiful gardens and traditional architecture.

• Return to Chiang Mai or Extend Your Trip

After a fulfilling day of exploring Chiang Rai and the Golden Triangle, it's time to head back to Chiang Mai. The drive back offers a chance to relax and reflect on your travels. Once you arrive in Chiang Mai, you may choose to extend your trip with additional activities or simply unwind at your hotel.

If you decide to extend your stay, Chiang Mai offers plenty of options, including cooking classes, visits to elephant sanctuaries, or exploring more temples and markets. The choices are endless, and the warm atmosphere of the city makes it an inviting place to linger.

Chapter Seven: Practical Information & Resources for Travelers

Recommended accommodations

Here's a detailed overview of recommended accommodations in Vietnam, Cambodia, Laos, and Northern Thailand, categorized by luxury, mid-range, and budget options.

• **Recommended Accommodations**

• **Vietnam**

1. Hanoi

- **Luxury: Sofitel Legend Metropole Hanoi**

A historic hotel with French colonial charm located in the heart of the city. It offers elegant rooms, fine dining, and a luxurious spa.

- Mid-Range: Hanoi La Siesta Hotel & Spa

This hotel combines modern comfort with traditional Vietnamese design. Guests enjoy cozy rooms, a spa, and a rooftop bar with great views.

- Budget: Little Hanoi Diamond Hotel

A charming and affordable option in the Old Quarter, this hotel provides clean rooms and friendly service, perfect for budget travelers.

2. Ho Chi Minh City (Saigon)

- Luxury: The Reverie Saigon

This luxurious hotel features stunning decor, gourmet restaurants, and a prime location along the Saigon River.

- Mid-Range: Hotel Nikko Saigon

Offering spacious rooms and great amenities, this hotel is known for its hospitality and convenient location.

- Budget: Duc Vuong Hotel

A popular choice among backpackers, this hotel provides clean and comfortable rooms with a friendly atmosphere.

• **Cambodia**

3. Phnom Penh

- Luxury: Rosewood Phnom Penh

This five-star hotel offers breathtaking views of the city, luxurious rooms, a spa, and excellent dining options.

- Mid-Range: Palace Gate Hotel

Close to the Royal Palace, this hotel combines modern comforts with a touch of Cambodian tradition.

- Budget: The Daun Penh Hotel

An affordable hotel located in the Riverside area, providing comfortable rooms and a welcoming atmosphere.

4. Siem Reap

- Luxury: Anantara Angkor Resort & Spa

An elegant resort that offers luxury accommodations, a beautiful pool, and a spa, perfect for relaxation after temple visits.

- Mid-Range: Jasmine Lodge

A cozy hotel that offers comfortable rooms, friendly staff, and easy access to the Angkor Wat complex.

- Budget: Happy Guesthouse

A budget-friendly option with a laid-back atmosphere, offering simple rooms and a communal area for travelers to meet.

• **Laos**

5. Luang Prabang

- Luxury: Belmond La Résidence Phou Vao

Set on a hillside, this luxury hotel offers stunning views, an infinity pool, and a serene spa.

- Mid-Range: Villa Maly

This boutique hotel blends modern comforts with colonial charm, located near the city center.

- Budget: Vang Thong Hotel

An affordable option in a great location, offering clean rooms and easy access to local attractions.

6. Vientiane

- Luxury: Settha Palace Hotel

A beautiful colonial-style hotel with luxurious rooms, a pool, and a fine dining restaurant.

- Mid-Range: Vientiane Plaza Hotel

This is a modern hotel with bar and a great view of the city.

- Budget: Manorom Boutique Hotel

A friendly guesthouse with affordable rates, providing basic amenities and a welcoming atmosphere.

• **Northern Thailand**

7. Chiang Mai

- Luxury: Four Seasons Resort Chiang Mai

A stunning resort set amidst rice paddies, offering luxurious villas, a world-class spa, and fine dining options.

- Mid-Range: U Nimman Chiang Mai

A stylish hotel with modern amenities, located near shopping and dining options in the trendy Nimman area.

- Budget: Green Tiger House

A budget-friendly guesthouse with a relaxed vibe, offering comfortable rooms and a communal area for socializing.

8. Chiang Rai

- Mid-Range: Teak Garden Lodge

This charming lodge features comfortable rooms and beautiful gardens, located near the city center.

- Budget: Singing Bird Homestay

An affordable and cozy option, providing simple rooms and a warm, welcoming environment.

Local transportation options

Traveling around Vietnam, Cambodia, Laos, and Northern Thailand can be an adventure in itself. Each country offers various transportation options to help you navigate and explore their unique landscapes and vibrant cities.

1. Buses

- Vietnam

Here, buses are a popular. It's as also affordable for people and travelers. There are different types, from local buses to sleeper buses for overnight trips. Major companies include Phuong Trang and Sinh Tourist.

- Cambodia

Buses connect cities like Phnom Penh, Siem Reap, and Sihanoukville. Giant Ibis and Mekong Express are well-known for their comfort and reliability.

- Laos

Buses are available for intercity travel, with varying levels of comfort. The local minivans, or "songthaews," are also a common way to get around.

- Northern Thailand

Buses run regularly between cities like Chiang Mai and Chiang Rai, with both government and private options. The Green Bus Company is a popular choice.

2. Trains

- Vietnam

The North-South Railway offers scenic train rides between Hanoi and Ho Chi Minh City.

Trains can be a comfortable way to see the countryside.

- Cambodia

There are limited train services, but a route from Phnom Penh to Sihanoukville has recently been revived.

- Laos

Train travel is still developing, with the Vientiane to Boten railway connecting Laos to China. It's a new experience for travelers.

- Northern Thailand

Trains run between major cities, including Bangkok and Chiang Mai. They offer various classes, from basic seats to luxury sleeper cars.

3. Flights

- Vietnam

Domestic flights are widely available between major cities, such as Hanoi, Ho Chi Minh City, and Da Nang.

Airlines like VietJet Air and Vietnam Airlines offer competitive prices.

- Cambodia

Flights connect Phnom Penh and Siem Reap with nearby countries and some domestic routes.

- Laos

Domestic flights are available between Vientiane, Luang Prabang, and Pakse, mainly operated by Lao Airlines.

- Northern Thailand

Chiang Mai has flights connecting to Bangkok and other regional destinations, making air travel a convenient option.

4. Tuk-Tuks

- Vietnam

Commonly found in cities like Ho Chi Minh City and Hanoi, tuk-tuks (often called "xe om") are a fun and easy way to get around short distances.

- Cambodia

Tuk-tuks are a popular choice in cities like Phnom Penh and Siem Reap. They are typically affordable and can be hired for a whole day.

- Laos

Tuk-tuks are available in Luang Prabang and Vientiane, often used for short trips around town.

- Northern Thailand

Tuk-tuks are a familiar sight in Chiang Mai and other cities, providing a quick way to travel short distances.

5. Taxis

- Vietnam

Metered taxis are widely available, especially in major cities. Grab, a ridesharing app, is also popular for booking rides.

- Cambodia

Taxis are available but less common than tuk-tuks. Grab can also be used for convenience.

- Laos

Taxis are available in Vientiane, but it's more common to use tuk-tuks or songthaews.

- Northern Thailand

Taxis are metered and found in major cities, while ridesharing apps like Grab are increasingly popular.

Key phrases in Vietnamese, Khmer, Lao, and Thai

Knowing a few key phrases in the local languages can enhance your travel experience. Here are some useful phrases in Vietnamese, Khmer (the language of Cambodia), Lao, and Thai.

• **Vietnamese (Tiếng Việt)**

- **Hello:** Xin chào

- **Thank you:** Cảm ơn

- **Yes:** Có

- **No:** Không

- **How much is this?:** Cái này bao nhiêu tiền?

- **Where is…?:** …ở đâu?

- **Help!:** Giúp tôi với!

- **Khmer (ខ្មែរ)**

- **Hello:** សួស្ដី (Susadei)

- **Thank you:** អរគុណ (Arkun)

- **Yes:** បាទ (Bat) for males / ចាស (Chas) for females

- **No:** ទេ (Te)

- **How much is this?:** តើនេះមានតម្លៃប៉ុន្មាន? (Tae nih mean tamlai ponman?)

- **Where is...?:** ...នៅឯណា? (...nov ae na?)

- **Help!:** ជួយផង! (Chouy phang!)

- **Lao (ລາວ)**

- **Hello:** ສະບາຍດ (Sabaidee)

- **Thank you:** ຂອບໃຈ (Khob chai)

- **Yes:** ບ (Bor)

- **No:** ບໍ່ (Bor)

- **How much is this?:** ນີ້ມີລາຄາແມ່ນດ໋ອໃດ? (Nii mi lakha man diao dai?)

- **Where is...?:** ...ຍູ່ໃສ? (...yuu sai?)

- **Help!:** ຊ່ອຍຂໍ! (Soi kho!)

• **Thai (ไทย)**

- **Hello:** สวัสดี (Sawasdee)

- **Thank you:** ขอบคุณ (Khop khun)

- **Yes:** ใช่ (Chai)

- **No:** ไม่ (Mai)

- **How much is this?:** อันนี้ราคาเท่าไหร่? (An ni rakha thao rai?)

- **Where is...?:** ...อยู่ที่ไหน? (...yuu thi nai?)

- **Help!:** ช่วยด้วย! (Chuay duay!)

Packing guide for Southeast Asia

Packing for a trip to Southeast Asia requires a balance between comfort, practicality, and cultural sensitivity.

Here's a comprehensive list to help you prepare for your adventure:

• **Clothing**

- Lightweight, breathable fabrics

The weather in Southeast Asia is generally hot and humid. Choose clothes made from cotton or linen that allow your skin to breathe.

- Modest attire

When visiting temples or rural areas, wear clothes that cover your shoulders and knees. Consider packing a light shawl or scarf for added coverage.

- Comfortable footwear

Bring comfortable sandals for walking and flip-flops for the beach or hostel stays. If you plan on hiking, consider sturdy shoes or trail runners.

- Swimwear

Don't forget your swimsuit for beach days or hotel pools, but remember to wear a cover-up when leaving the beach.

- Light jacket or sweater

A lightweight jacket is useful for cooler evenings or when visiting higher altitudes.

• Accessories

- Sunglasses and sunhat

Protect yourself from the sun's rays with a good pair of sunglasses and a wide-brimmed hat.

- Daypack

A small backpack is handy for day trips, hikes, or visits to cities.

• **Toiletries and Health Supplies**

- **Basic toiletries**

Many hotels provide some amenities, but having your own can be convenient.

- **Insect repellent**

Mosquitoes can be prevalent, especially in rural areas. So, a good repellent is an important thing you should not omit.

• **Electronics**

- **Universal power adapter**

Southeast Asia uses various plug types, so a universal adapter is essential for charging devices.

- **Smartphone and portable charger**

A smartphone is useful for navigation, communication, and taking photos.

Download offline maps and relevant travel apps before your trip.

Health tips

Here are some tips to keep you healthy during your journey:

• **Health Tips**

- Vaccinations

Check with your doctor about recommended vaccinations for the countries or regions you are visiting. Common ones may include any of these: Typhoid, Tetanus or Hepatitis A.

- Drink bottled or filtered water

Tap water may not be safe to drink. Stick to bottled water and avoid ice in drinks unless you are sure it was made from safe water.

- Food safety

Street food is popular, but make sure to choose vendors that cook food fresh and have a good turnover. If in doubt, eat at busy places with high customer traffic.

- Be cautious of mosquitoes

Use insect repellent and wear long sleeves and pants in the evenings to reduce the risk of mosquito-borne diseases.

Additional resources

Below are some important websites and apps you may need to consider for your visit:

• **Websites**

- TripAdvisor

Offers reviews of hotels, restaurants, and attractions, helping you find the best options.

- Rome2rio

A useful site for finding transportation options between locations, including buses, trains, and flights.

• **Apps**

- Google Maps

For navigation purposes.

- Grab

A ridesharing app popular in Southeast Asia for taxis and food delivery.

- Duolingo

A fun way to learn basic phrases in Vietnamese, Khmer, Lao, and Thai before your trip.

OTHER BOOKS RECOMMENDATION

Dear Reader,

If you liked this guide, **Jude** suggests checking out his other books you might want to add to your reading list.

Thank you for being a valued reader! He looks forward to accompanying you on many more literary journeys.

A KIND GESTURE

Dear Fellow Travelers,

Your feedback on the guide is important to **Jude**. If it made your **trip** more magical, he'd appreciate it if you left a review and shared your experience with others. By spreading the word, you'll help fellow travelers have amazing adventures too.

Thank you for being part of this community of great adventurers. Your kind gesture in leaving a review and recommending the guide is a meaningful contribution to the shared joy of exploration.

Safe travels and happy exploring!
Jude K. Bremner

TRAVEL NOTE

TRAVEL NOTE

TRAVEL NOTE

TRAVEL NOTE

TRAVEL NOTE

TRAVEL NOTE

TRAVEL NOTE

TRAVEL NOTE

TRAVEL NOTE

TRAVEL NOTE